Learning Unix for
Mac OS X Panther

Other Macintosh resources from O'Reilly

Related titles

AppleWorks 6: The Missing Manual

Mac OS X Panther Pocket Guide

Mac OS X for Unix Geeks

Mac OS X Hacks

Mac OS X Hints

Mac OS X in a Nutshell

Mac OS X: The Missing Manual

Macintosh Books Resource Center

mac.oreilly.com is a complete catalog of O'Reilly's books on the Apple Macintosh and related technologies, including sample chapters and code examples.

A popular watering hole for Macintosh developers and power users, the Mac DevCenter focuses on pure Mac OS X and its related technologies, including Cocoa, Java, AppleScript, and Apache, to name just a few. It's also keenly interested in all the spokes of the digital hub, with special attention paid to digital photography, digital video, MP3 music, and QuickTime.

Conferences

O'Reilly & Associates brings diverse innovators together to nurture the ideas that spark revolutionary industries. We specialize in documenting the latest tools and systems, translating the innovator's knowledge into useful skills for those in the trenches. Visit *conferences.oreilly.com* for our upcoming events.

Safari Bookshelf (*safari.oreilly.com*) is the premier online reference library for programmers and IT professionals. Conduct searches across more than 1,000 books. Subscribers can zero in on answers to time-critical questions in a matter of seconds. Read the books on your Bookshelf from cover to cover or simply flip to the page you need. Try it today with a free trial.

Learning Unix for Mac OS X Panther

Dave Taylor and Brian Jepson

O'REILLY®

Beijing · Cambridge · Farnham · Köln · Paris · Sebastopol · Taipei · Tokyo

Learning Unix for Mac OS X Panther
by Dave Taylor and Brian Jepson

Copyright © 2004, 2003, 2002 O'Reilly Media, Inc. The previous editions of this book were titled *Learning Unix for Mac OS X*. All rights reserved. Printed in the United States of America.

Published by O'Reilly Media, Inc., 1005 Gravenstein Highway North, Sebastopol, CA 95472.

O'Reilly Media, Inc. books may be purchased for educational, business, or sales promotional use. Online editions are also available for most titles (*safari.oreilly.com*). For more information, contact our corporate/institutional sales department: (800) 998-9938 or *corporate@oreilly.com*.

Editor:	Nathan Torkington
Production Editor:	Mary Brady
Cover Designer:	Emma Colby
Interior Designer:	David Futato

Printing History:

May 2002:	First Edition.
January 2003:	Second Edition.
December 2003:	Third Edition.

 This book uses RepKover™, a durable and flexible lay-flat binding.

ISBN: 0-596-00617-9

[M]   [8/04]

Table of Contents

Preface

Mac OS X (pronounced "Mac OS Ten"), the latest incarnation of the Macintosh operating system, is a radical departure from previous versions. Not only is there a whole new look and feel on the surface, there are also huge differences under the hood. All the old, familiar Macintosh system software has been replaced with another operating system, called Unix. Unix is a multiuser, multitasking operating system. Being *multiuser* means Mac OS X allows multiple users to share the same system, each having the ability to customize their desktop, create files that can be kept private from other users, and make settings that will automatically be restored whenever that person uses the computer. Being *multitasking* means Mac OS X can easily run many different applications at the same time, and that if one application crashes or hangs, the entire system doesn't need to be rebooted.

The fact that Mac OS X is Unix under the hood doesn't matter to users who simply want to use its slick graphical interface to run their applications or manage their files. But it opens up worlds of possibilities for users who want to dig a little deeper. The Unix command-line interface, which is accessible through a Mac application in the Utilities folder called Terminal, provides an enormous amount of power for intermediate and advanced users. What's more, once you've learned to use Unix in Mac OS X, you'll also be able to use the command line in other versions of Unix or the Unix-compatible Linux.

This book is designed to teach the basics of Unix to Macintosh users. We tell you how to use the command line (which Unix users refer to as "the shell") and the filesystem, as well as some of the most useful commands. Unix is a complex and powerful system, so we scratch only the surface, but we also tell you how to deepen your Unix knowledge once you're ready for more.

Audience

This book teaches basic system utility commands to get you started with Unix. Instead of overwhelming you with lots of details, we want you to be comfortable in the Unix environment as soon as possible. So we cover each command's most useful features instead of describing all its options in detail.

We also assume that your computer works properly; you have started it, know the procedure for turning the power off, and know how to perform system maintenance.

Who This Book Is Not For

If you're seeking a book that talks about how to develop Cocoa programs or otherwise build Mac software applications, this isn't your book (though it's quite helpful for developers to have a good grasp of Mac OS X Unix essentials). If you're a complete beginner and are occasionally stymied by where the second mouse button went, this might be a better book to put on the shelf until you're more comfortable with your computing environment. Finally, if you live and breathe Unix every day and can make your Linux box do backflips, this book will be too basic for you (though, since we cover many of the Mac OS X Unix nuances, you'll still glean information from reading it). We don't cover either Unix system administration or Mac system administration from the command line.

A Brief History

The Macintosh started out with a single-tasking operating system that allowed simple switching between applications through an application called the Finder. More recent versions of Mac OS have supported multiple applications running simultaneously, but it wasn't until the landmark release of Mac OS X that true multitasking arrived in the Macintosh world. With Mac OS X, Macintosh applications run in separate memory areas; the Mac is a true multiuser system that also finally includes proper file-level security.

To accomplish these improvements, Mac OS X made the jump from a proprietary underlying operating environment to Unix. Mac OS X is built on top of Darwin, a version of Unix based on BSD 4.4 Lite, FreeBSD, NetBSD, and the Mach microkernel.

Unix itself was invented more than 30 years ago for scientific and professional users who wanted a very powerful and flexible OS. It has evolved since then through a remarkably circuitous path, with stops at Bell Telephone Labs, UC Berkeley, research centers in Australia and Europe, and the U.S. Department of Defense Advanced Research Projects Agency (for funding). Because Unix was designed for experts, it can be a bit overwhelming at first. But after you get the basics (from this book!), you'll start to appreciate some of the reasons to use Unix:

- It comes with a huge number of powerful application programs. You can get many others for free on the Internet. (The Fink project, available from SourceForge (*http://fink.sourceforge.net/*), brings many open source packages to Mac OS X.) You can thus do much more at a much lower cost. Another place to explore is the cool DarwinPorts project, where a dedicated team of software developers are creating Darwin versions of many popular Unix apps (*http://www.opendarwin.org/projects/darwinports*).

- Not only are the applications often free, but so are some Unix (and Unix-compatible) operating systems. Linux and FreeBSD are good examples. Like the free applications, most free Unix versions are of excellent quality. They're maintained by volunteer programmers and corporations who want a powerful OS and are frustrated by the slow, bug-ridden OS development at some big software companies. Mac OS X's Darwin core is a free Unix OS (get it at *http://developer.apple.com/darwin/*), but it does not have Mac OS X's easy-to-use interface. Many people use Mac OS X daily without ever knowing about all the power lurking under the hood.

- Unix runs on almost any kind of computer, from tiny embedded systems to giant supercomputers. After you read this book, you'll not only know all about Darwin, but you'll also be ready to use many other kinds of Unix-based computers without learning a new OS for each one.

- In general, Unix (especially without a windowing system) is less resource intensive than other major operating systems. For instance, Linux will run happily on an old system with an Intel 80386 microprocessor and let multiple users share the same computer. (Don't bother trying to use the latest versions of Microsoft Windows on a system that's more than a few years old!) If you need a windowing system, Unix lets you choose from modern feature-rich interfaces as well as from simple ones that need much less system power. Anyone with limited resources—educational institutions, organizations in developing countries, and so on—can use Unix to do more with less.

- Much of the Internet's development was done on Unix systems. Many Internet web sites and service providers use Unix because it's so flexible and inexpensive. With powerful hardware, Unix really shines.

Versions of Unix

There are several versions of Unix. Some past and present commercial versions include Solaris, AIX, and HP/UX. Freely available versions include Linux, NetBSD, OpenBSD, and FreeBSD. Darwin, the free Unix underneath Mac OS X, was built by grafting an advanced version called Mach onto BSD, with a light sprinkling of Apple magic for the windowing system.

Although graphical user interfaces (GUIs) and advanced features differ among Unix systems, you should be able to use much of what you learn from this introductory handbook on any system. Don't worry too much about what's from what version of Unix. Just as English borrows words from French, German, Japanese, Italian, and even Hebrew, Mac OS X Unix borrows commands from many different versions of Unix, and you can use them all without paying attention to their origins.

From time to time, we do explain features of Unix on other systems. Knowing the differences can help you if you ever want to use another type of Unix system. When we write "Unix" in this book, we mean "Unix and its versions," unless we specifically mention a particular version.

Interfaces to Unix

Unix can be used as it was originally designed: on typewriter-like terminals, from a prompt on a command line. Most versions of Unix also work with window systems (or GUIs). These allow each user to have a single screen with multiple windows—including "terminal" windows that act like the original Unix interface.

Mac OS X includes a simple terminal application for accessing the command-line level of the system. That application, reasonably enough, is called Terminal and can be found in the Applications → Utilities folder. The Terminal application will be examined more closely in Chapters 1 and 2.

Although you can certainly use your Mac quite efficiently without typing text at a shell prompt, we'll spend all our time in this book on that traditional command-line interface to Unix. Why?

- Every Unix system has a command-line interface. If you know how to use the command line, you'll always be able to use the system.

- If you become a more advanced Unix user, you'll find that the command line is actually much more flexible than a windowing interface. Unix programs are designed to be used together from the command line—as "building blocks"—in an almost infinite number of combinations, to do an infinite number of tasks. No windowing system we've seen (yet!) has this tremendous power.

- You can launch and close GUI programs from the command line.

- Once you learn to use the command line, you can use those same techniques to write *scripts*. These little (or big!) programs automate jobs you'd have to do manually and repetitively with a window system (unless you understand how to program a window system, which is usually a much harder job). See the section "Programming" in Chapter 10 for a brief introduction to scripting.

- In general, text-based interfaces are much easier than GUIs for sight-impaired users.

We aren't saying that the command-line interface is right for every situation. For instance, using the Web—with its graphics and links—is usually easier with a GUI web browser within Mac OS X. But the command line is the fundamental way to use Unix. Understanding it will let you work on any Unix system, with or without windows. A great resource for general Mac OS X information (the GUI you're probably used to) can be found in *Mac OS X: The Missing Manual* by David Pogue (Pogue Press/O'Reilly).

Conventions Used in This Book

The following typographical conventions are used in this book:

Plain text
> Indicates menu titles, menu options, menu buttons, and keyboard accelerators (such as Alt and Ctrl).

Italic
> Indicates new terms, URLs, email addresses, filenames, file extensions, pathnames, directories, and Unix utilities.

`Constant width`
> Indicates commands, options, switches, variables, attributes, keys, functions, types, classes, namespaces, methods, modules, properties, parameters, values, objects, events, event handlers, XML tags, HTML tags, macros, the contents of files, or the output from commands.

`Constant width bold`
> Shows commands or other text that should be typed literally by the user.

`Constant width italic`
> Shows text that should be replaced with user-supplied values.

This icon signifies a tip, suggestion, or general note.

 This icon indicates a warning or caution.

Using Code Examples

This book is here to help you get your job done. In general, you may use the code in this book in your programs and documentation. You do not need to contact us for permission unless you're reproducing a significant portion of the code. For example, writing a program that uses several chunks of code from this book does not require permission. Selling or distributing a CD-ROM of examples from O'Reilly books does require permission. Answering a question by citing this book and quoting example code does not require permission. Incorporating a significant amount of example code from this book into your product's documentation does require permission.

We appreciate, but do not require, attribution. An attribution usually includes the title, author, publisher, and ISBN. For example: "*Learning Unix for Mac OS X Panther,* Third Edition, by Dave Taylor and Brian Jepson. Copyright 2004 O'Reilly & Associates, Inc., 0-596-00617-9."

If you feel your use of code examples falls outside fair use or the permission given above, feel free to contact us at *permissions@oreilly.com.*

Comments and Questions

Please address comments and questions concerning this book to the publisher:

> O'Reilly & Associates, Inc.
> 1005 Gravenstein Highway North
> Sebastopol, CA 95472
> (800) 998-9938 (in the United States or Canada)
> (707) 829-0515 (international or local)
> (707) 829-0104 (fax)

We have a web page for this book, where we list errata, examples, and any additional information. You can access this page at:

> *http://www.oreilly.com/catalog/lunixpanther*

To comment or ask technical questions about this book, send email to:

bookquestions@oreilly.com

For more information about our books, conferences, Resource Centers, and the O'Reilly Network, see our web site at:

http://www.oreilly.com

The Evolution of This Book

This book is based on the popular O'Reilly title *Learning the Unix Operating System*, by Jerry Peek, Grace Todino, and John Strang (currently in its fifth edition). There are many differences in this book to meet the needs of Mac OS X users, but the fundamental layout and explanations are the same.

Acknowledgments for Dave Taylor

I'd like to acknowledge the great work of Nat Torkington, our editor at O'Reilly, and the valuable information and review of the manuscript by Apple Computer, Inc. I would also like to express my gratitude to Chuck Toporek for his valuable comments on the draft manuscript. Thanks also to Christian Crumlish for his back-room assistance, and to Tim O'Reilly for the opportunity to help revise the popular *Learning the Unix Operating System* book for the exciting new Mac OS X world. Oh, and a big thumbs up to Linda, Ashley, Gareth, and "Peanut" for letting me type, type, and type some more, ultimately getting this book out the door in a remarkably speedy manner.

Acknowledgments for Brian Jepson

I'd like to thank Nathan Torkington, my editor, for helping me shape, launch, and complete this project. Thanks also to Chuck Toporek, who gave us lots of guidance on where to take this next edition. Special thanks to Joan, Seiji, and Yeuhi for their patience as I slipped away into various corners of the house to work on this book.

## CHAPTER 1

Getting Into Unix

One of the great pleasures of using Unix with Mac OS X surrounding it is that you get the benefit of a truly wonderful graphical application environment and the underlying power of the raw Unix interface. A match made in heaven!

This chapter explains the how and the why: how to customize your Terminal environment both from the graphical user interface using Terminal → Window Settings and from the Unix shell by using shell configuration files, and why you'd want to use Unix in the first place. Let's start with the question of why, shall we?

Why Use Unix?

It's an obvious question, particularly if you're a long-time Macintosh person who is familiar and happy with the capabilities and logic of the graphical world, with its Aqua interface built on top of the Quartz rendering system. Dipping into the primarily text-based Unix tools on your Mac OS X system can give you even greater power and control over both your computer and your computing environment. There are other reasons, including that it's fun and there are thousands of open source and otherwise freely downloadable Unix-based applications, particularly for science and engineering. But, fundamentally, it's all about *power* and *control*.

As an example, consider the difference between the graphical *Force Quit* option on the Apple menu and the Unix programs ps and kill. While *Force Quit* is more attractive, as shown in Figure 1-1, notice that it lists only a very small number of applications.

By contrast, the ps (*processor status*) command used from within the Terminal application (Applications → Utilities → Terminal) shows a complete and

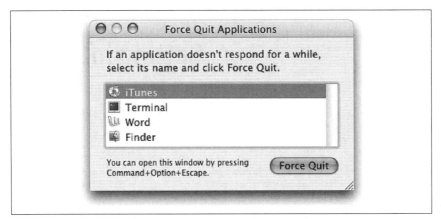

Figure 1-1. Force Quit doesn't show all running applications

full list of every application, utility, and system process running on the computer:

```
$ ps -ax
  PID  TT  STAT     TIME COMMAND
    1  ??  Ss    0:00.04 /sbin/init
    2  ??  Ss    0:00.19 /sbin/mach_init
   78  ??  Ss    0:00.18 /usr/sbin/syslogd -s -m 0
   84  ??  Ss    0:02.67 kextd
   86  ??  Ss    0:01.51 /usr/sbin/configd
   87  ??  Ss    0:01.12 /usr/sbin/diskarbitrationd
...
  358 std  Ss    0:00.03 login -pf taylor
  359 std  S     0:00.04 -bash
  361 std  R+    0:00.01 ps ax
```

Quite a few applications, certainly many more than *Force Quit* suggests, are running. This is the key reason to learn and work with the Unix side of Mac OS X in addition to the attractive graphical facet of the operating system: to really know what's going on and be able to make it match what you want and need.

Here's another example. Suppose you just received a CD-ROM from a client with a few hundred files all in the main folder. You need to copy to your home directory just those files that have "-nt-" or "-dt-" as part of their filenames. Within the Finder, you'd be doomed to going through the list manually, a tedious and error-prone process. On the Unix command line, it'd be a breeze:

```
$ cd /Volumes/MyCDROM
$ cp *-dt-* *-nt-* ~
```

Fast, easy, and doable by any and all Mac OS X users.

There are a million reasons why it's helpful to know Unix as a Mac OS X power user, and you'll see them demonstrated time and again throughout this book. They are shown in even more detail in advanced books like *Mac OS X Panther for Unix Geeks*, by Brian Jepson and Ernest E. Rothman (O'Reilly).

Launching Terminal

Launch Terminal by moving to the Applications folder in the Finder, opening up Utilities, and then double-clicking on the Terminal application, as shown in Figure 1-2. It starts up and you have a dull, uninspiring, white window with black text that says "Welcome to Darwin!", and a shell prompt.

Figure 1-2. Finding Terminal in the Utilities folder

 By default, Terminal uses bash as its shell. If you'd like to configure it to use a different shell, you can do so by selecting Terminal → Preferences and specifying the shell to use. We talk about that later in this chapter in the section "Shell."

Changing Terminal Preferences

To change the Terminal's preferences, go to Terminal → Window Settings....
You see a display similar to Figure 1-3.

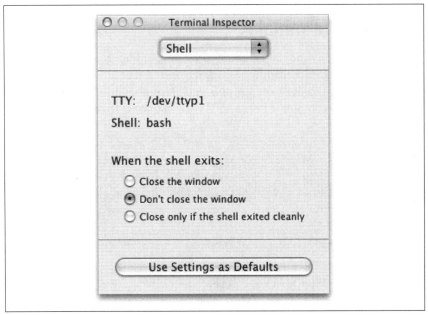

Figure 1-3. Shell settings

At the top of the window, notice that a drop-down list lets you select which options to configure: Shell, Processes, Emulation, Buffer, Display, Color, Window, and Keyboard. The names suggest what each does, but let's have a closer look anyway, particularly since some of these settings definitely *should* be changed in our view.

Any changes you make within the Terminal Inspector will affect only the current Terminal window unless you click "Use Settings as Defaults," after which they will apply to all future Terminal windows that you open.

Shell

When you first open the Terminal Inspector, the Shell settings are displayed, as shown in Figure 1-3. This panel specifies which tty (virtual Terminal device) and shell are associated with the current Terminal window. In addition, it allows you to choose one of the following options: when a login shell exits, the Terminal application can close the window; close the window only if the shell exited cleanly (that is, returned a zero status code, which means that all the applications gracefully shut down); or never close the window. If you like to study what you've done and want to be forced to explicitly close the Terminal window, "Don't close the window" is for you. Otherwise, either of the other two will work fine.

If you want to change the login shell for future Terminal windows, open up the Terminal → Preferences dialog box, as shown in Figure 1-4.

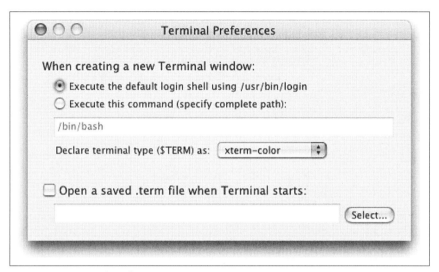

Figure 1-4. Terminal Preferences

Almost all users will leave these preferences alone. The most interesting of them is the option of opening a saved *.term* file: we'll talk about *.term* files later in this chapter in the section "Working with .term Files."

Processes

One of the more subtle capabilities of the Terminal application is that it can keep track of what applications you're running so it can be smart about confirming window close requests: if there's something still running in the window, a dialog box pops up asking if you're sure you want to quit. This feature is very helpful if you are prone to accidentally clicking the wrong window element or pushing the wrong key sequence.

The Processes window shown in Figure 1-5 lists all the processes running under the Terminal window and lets you specify what to do when you close a window. Set "Prompt before closing window" to "Always" if you'd like Terminal to always ask before closing the window, or set it to "Never" to prevent it from ever asking. You can also use "If there are processes other than" setting (the default) to ignore the programs shown in the list (you can add or remove items from this list).

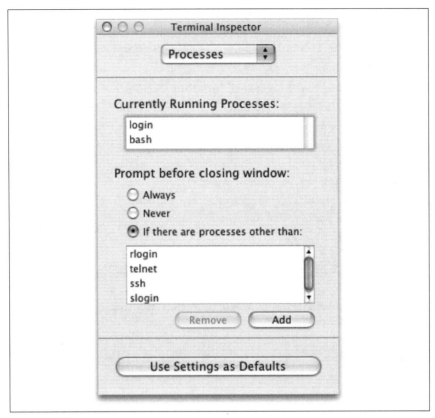

Figure 1-5. Processes

Emulation

These preferences, shown in Figure 1-6, don't need to be altered by most users.

 Some PowerBook G4s have a long delay before emitting audio. If you have one of these and you feel it's a problem, deselect "Audible bell" to neatly sidestep the issue. This also has a nice side effect of preventing people around you knowing when you've made a mistake.

It's best to leave "Paste newlines as carriage returns" so that you can ignore the difference in end-of-line sequences in Mac files versus Unix files, and to avoid strict "VT-100" emulation because it can get in the way of some of the newer Mac OS X Unix utilities. Whether you enable "Option click to position cursor" might depend on whether you're a Unix purist (for whom the "good old keyboard" works fine) or whether you're trying to simplify things.

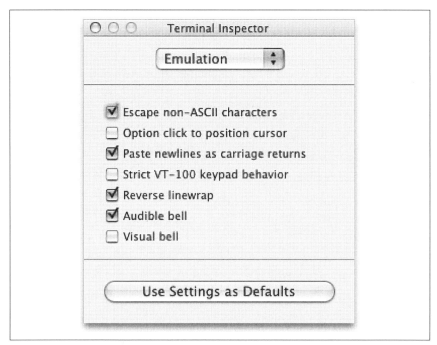

Figure 1-6. Emulation

Beware that if you do enable Option-click positioning, it won't work in all cases—only when you're in a full-screen application such as Emacs or vi.

Buffer

The settings in this area probably don't need changing, as shown in Figure 1-7. The scrollback buffer allows you to scroll back and review earlier commands and command output. The default value of 10,000 lines should be more than enough for most people. If you want to use less memory, you can put in a smaller number or completely disable the scrollback buffer, rather than specify a size.

You can also choose whether the Terminal should wrap long lines (not all Unix programs will wrap long lines, and might disappear off the edge of the window if this option isn't set), or whether you should automatically jump to the bottom of the scroll buffer upon input (if you've scrolled back to examine something that transpired earlier in your session). These options are set by default, and you should probably leave them that way.

Display

One area that you'll probably fine-tune more than others is Display, as shown in Figure 1-8. Here you can specify a different (or larger) font, define

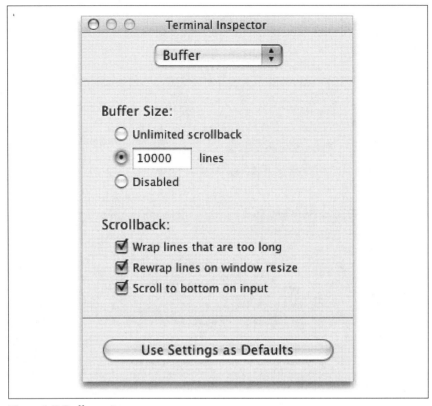

Figure 1-7. Buffer settings

the shape of your cursor within the Terminal window, and control character set encoding.

While you can choose any font available on your system, you'll find that your display will end up quite wonky and unreadable if you don't stick with monospace or fixed-width typefaces. Monaco is a good choice, and is the default typeface for the Terminal application.

Finally, you can specify a nonstandard string encoding if you're working with an unusual language or font. The default UTF-8 (Unicode 8-bit) encoding will work in most situations.

Color

The Color settings let you change the normal text, background, bold text, cursor, and selection colors, as well set the transparency of your Terminal window. The default color settings display black text on a white background, but we find that light text on a dark background is easier to read for

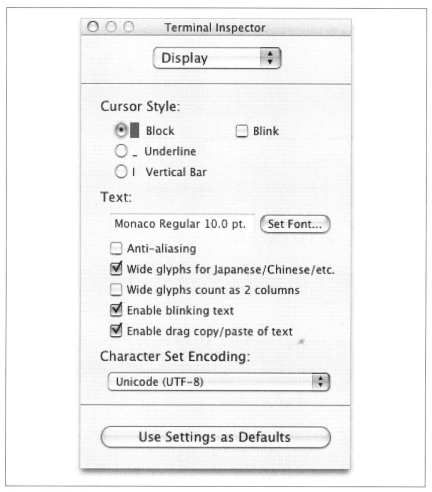

Figure 1-8. Display settings

extended periods. One suggested setting is to have the background very dark blue, the cursor yellow, normal text light yellow, bold text light green, and the selection dark green. The default color scheme is black text on a white background, as shown in Figure 1-9.

It's worth experimenting with the different predefined color settings. We particularly like green on black and white on blue, but your tastes will undoubtedly vary!

Window

If you have a large display or are running at a higher resolution than 800×600, you'll find it quite helpful to enlarge the Terminal window to offer a bigger

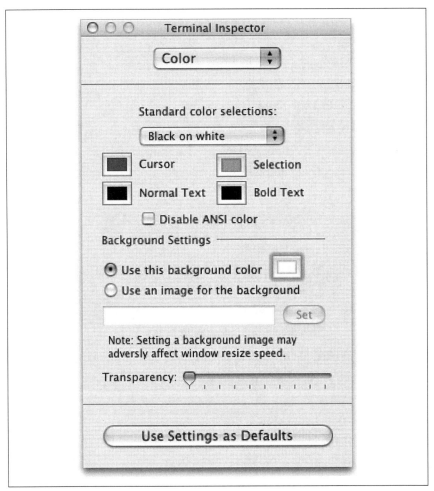

Figure 1-9. Color settings

space within which to work. The default is 80 characters wide by 24 lines tall, as shown in Figure 1-10.

The title of each Terminal window can be fine-tuned as well. You might find the device name (what you'd get if you typed **tty** at the shell prompt), the window dimensions, and the Command Key option (this shows you which command sequence lets you jump directly to that Terminal window from any other Terminal window you might be using) all particularly helpful.

 If you want to change the Terminal window title at any point, you can use the Set Title option either by choosing it from the File menu or by typing ⌘-Shift-T.

Figure 1-10. Window preferences

Keyboard

The final Terminal Inspector pane is the Keyboard pane (see Figure 1-11), which offers much control over which key performs which function within the Unix environment. However, switching something without knowing how it's used can be quite problematic, so we recommend that you do not change any of these settings unless you know exactly what you're doing.

Customizing Your Shell Environment

The Unix shell reads a number of configuration files when it starts up. These configuration files are really *shell programs*, so they are extraordinarily

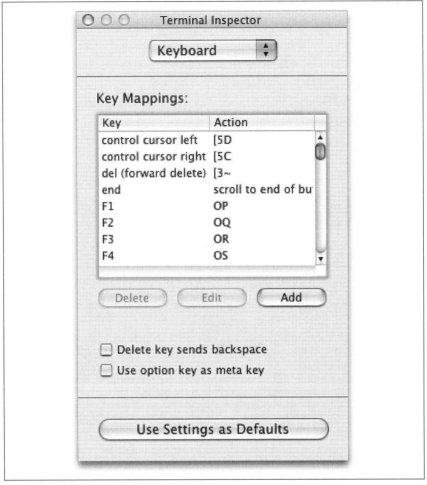

Figure 1-11. Keyboard preferences

powerful. Shell programming is beyond the scope of this book. For more detail, see Cameron Newham and Bill Rosenblatts' book *Learning the bash Shell* (O'Reilly) or Dave Taylors' *Wicked Cool Shell Scripts* (NoStarch). Because Unix is a multiuser system, there are two possible locations for the configuration files: one applies to all users of the system and another to each individual user.

The system-wide setup files that are read by *bash*, the default shell for Mac OS X, are found in */etc* (*profile* and *bashrc*). You only have permission to change these system-wide files if you use *sudo* (see "Superuser Privileges with sudo" in Chapter 3). However, you can create another file called *.profile* in your home directory that will add additional commands to be executed whenever you start a new Terminal window. (If you configure

Terminal to use another shell, such as the Bourne shell, the C shell, or the Z shell, you'll need to set up different configuration files. See the manpage for the appropriate shell for details.)

The system-wide setup files are read first, then the user-specific ones, so commands in your *.profile* file can override those in the system-wide files. The system-wide *profile* and *bashrc* files are succinct:

```
$ cat /etc/profile
# System-wide .profile for sh(1)

PATH="/bin:/sbin:/usr/bin:/usr/sbin"
export PATH

[ -r /etc/bashrc ] && source /etc/bashrc
$ cat /etc/bashrc
# System-wide .bashrc file for interactive bash(1) shells.
PS1='\h:\w \u\$ '
$
```

If you want to change the PATH for all users, perhaps to add */Developer/Tools* (see Chapter 4 for details on what you can find in that directory), modify the */etc/profile* contents thusly:

```
PATH="/bin:/sbin:/usr/bin:/usr/sbin:/Developer/Tools"
```

The *.profile* file can contain any shell command that you want to run automatically whenever you create a new Terminal. Some typical examples include changing the shell prompt, setting environment variables (values that control the operation of other Unix utilities), setting aliases, or adding to the search path (where the shell searches for programs to be run). A *.profile* file could look like this:

```
export PS1="\w (\!) : "
export LESS="eMq"
alias desktop="cd ~/Desktop"
date
```

This sample *.profile* file issues the following commands:

- The line that changes the value of PS1 tells the shell to use a different prompt than the standard one. We'll explain the details of prompt setting in the section "Changing Your Prompt" later in this chapter.

- The line with export LESS sets a shell variable that the less program recognizes to change its default behavior. In this case, it's identical to typing in **less -eMq** each time you use the command. Not all commands recognize environment variables, but for those that do, this saves you the trouble of typing the options on every less command line.

- The line that begins with alias defines a new, custom command that your shell will recognize just as if it were a built-in Unix command. Aliases are a great way to save shorthand names for long, complicated Unix command lines, or even to fix common mistakes you might make when typing command lines. This particular alias creates a command for going right to the Desktop directory. We give a brief tutorial on creating aliases later in this chapter in the section "Creating Aliases."

- The date line simply runs the date command to print the time and date when you open a new Terminal window. You probably don't want to do this, but we want you to understand that you can put in any command that you could type at the shell prompt and have it automatically executed whenever a new shell starts up.

By default, the *.profile* file doesn't exist in your home directory, and only the system-wide configuration files are read each time a Terminal window is opened. But if you create the file in your home directory, it will be read and its contents executed the next time you start a shell. You can create or change these files with a text editor, such as vi (see "The vi Text Editor" in Chapter 4). Don't use a word processor that breaks long lines or puts special nontext codes into the file. Any changes you make to these files will take effect when you open a new Terminal window. Unfortunately, it's not always easy to know which shell setup file you should change. And an editing mistake in your shell setup file can interfere with the normal startup of the Terminal window. We suggest that beginners get help from experienced users, and don't make changes to these files at all if you're about to do some critical work with your account, unless there's some reason you have to make the changes immediately.

You can execute any customization command we discuss here from the command line as well. In this case, the changes are in effect only until you close that window or quit Terminal.

For example, to change the default options for less so it will clear the Terminal window before it shows each new page of text, you could add the -c option to the LESS environment variable. The command would look something like this:

```
$ export LESS='eMqc'
```

(If you don't want some of the less options we've shown, you could leave those letters out.)

Unix has many other configuration commands to learn about; the sources listed in Chapter 10 can help you identify which modifications you can make and how they can help you produce an optimal computing environment for yourself.

Just as you can execute the setup commands from the command line, the converse is true: any command that you can execute from the command line can be executed automatically when you log in by placing it in your setup file. (Running interactive commands such as vi or ftp from your setup file isn't a good idea, though.)

Changing Your Prompt

The easiest customization you can perform is to change your prompt. By default, *bash* on Mac OS X has a shell prompt made up of your computer hostname, your current working directory, your account name, and a dollar sign (for example: Dave-Taylors-Computer:~ taylor$). If you'd rather have something else, it's time to edit your own *.bashrc* file. Use the vi editor (you might need to flip to "The vi Text Editor" in Chapter 4) to create a file called *.profile* in your home directory (*/Users/yourname*), and then add the following to the end of the file: **export PS1="$ "**. You can also change the prompt for a single session by invoking the command as follows:

```
Dave-Taylors-Computer:~ taylor$ PS1="$ "
$
```

This command will give you a simple, spare $ prompt with nothing else. (The % is traditional for shells derived from the Berkeley Unix C Shell, while $ is traditional for shells derived from the original Bell Labs Bourne Shell.) It's not necessary—you could use a colon, a greater-than sign, or any other prompt character—but it is a nice convention, because it will immediately tell an advanced user what kind of shell you are using.

If that's all you could do to set your prompt, it wouldn't be very interesting, though. There are a number of special character sequences that, when used to define the prompt, cause the shell to print out various bits of useful data. Table 1-1 shows a partial list of these special character sequences for fine-tuning your prompt.

Table 1-1. Favorite escape sequences for bash prompts

Value	Meaning
\w	The current working directory
\W	The trailing element of the current working directory, with ~ substitution
\!	The current command history number
\H	The full hostname
\h	The hostname up to the first dot
\@	Time of day in 12-hour (a.m./p.m.) format
\A	Time of day in 24-hour format

Table 1-1. Favorite escape sequences for bash prompts (continued)

Value	Meaning
\u	The username
\$	A # if the effective user ID is zero (root), or a $ otherwise

Experiment and see what you can create that will meet your needs and be fun too. For many years, a popular Unix prompt was:

```
$ PS1="Yes, Master? "
```

It might be a bit obsequious, but on the other hand, how many people in your life call you "Master"?

One prompt sequence that we like is:

```
$ PS1="\W \! \$ "
```

This prompt sequence shows the current working directory, followed by a space and the current history number, and then a $ or # to remind the user that this is *bash* and whether they're currently running as root. For example, the prompt might read:

```
/Users/taylor 55 $
```

This tells you immediately that */Users/taylor* is the current directory, and that you're on the 55th command you've executed. (Because you can use the arrow keys to scroll back to previous commands, as described in the section, "Recalling Previous Commands" in Chapter 2, this is no longer as important, but there is a very powerful command history syntax built into *bash* that allows you to recall a previous command by number. If you're familiar with this syntax, making the command history number part of the prompt can be handy.) On multiuser systems, it's not a bad idea to put the username into the prompt as well, so you always know who the system thinks you are.

Creating Aliases

The flexibility of Unix is simultaneously its greatest strength and downfall; the operating system can do just about anything you can imagine (the command-line interface is certainly far more flexible than the Finder!) but it's very difficult to remember every single flag to every command. That's where shell aliases can be a real boon. A shell alias is a simple mechanism that lets you create your own command names that act exactly as you desire.

For example, we really like the -a flag to be included every time we list a directory with ls, so we created an alias:

```
$ alias ls="/bin/ls -a"
```

This indicates that each time we type ls in the shell, the /bin/ls command is going to be run, and it's going to automatically have the -a flag specified. To have this available in your next session, make sure you remember to add the alias to your *.profile* file.

You can also have aliases that let you jump quickly to common locations, a particularly helpful trick when in Mac OS X:

```
$ alias desktop="cd ~/Desktop"
```

Chapter 4 describes the cp, mv, and rm commands, which copy, move, and remove files, respectively. Each of these support the -i switch, which will prompt you before overwriting or deleting a file. You can use aliases to always enable this switch:

```
$ alias rm="rm -i"
$ alias cp="cp -i"
$ alias mv="mv -i"
```

You can list active aliases all by typing alias without any arguments:

```
$ alias
alias cp='cp -i'
alias desktop='cd ~/Desktop'
alias ls='/bin/ls -a'
alias m2u='tr '\''\015'\'' '\''\012'\'''
alias u2m='tr '\''\012'\'' '\''\015'\'''
```

Have an alias you really want to omit? You can use unalias for that. For example, unalias ls would remove the -a flag addition.

Setting the Terminal Title

You can change the current Terminal title using the following cryptic sequence of characters:

```
echo '^[]2;My-Window-Title^G'
```

To type the ^[characters in *bash*, use the key sequence Control-V Escape (press Control-V and release, then press the Escape key). To type ^G, use Control-V Control-G. The vi editor supports the same key sequence.

Such cryptic sequences of characters are called *ANSI escape sequences*. An ANSI escape sequence is a special command that manipulates some characteristic of the Terminal, such as its title. ^[is the ASCII ESC character (which begins the sequence), and ^G is the ASCII BEL character. (The BEL character is used to ring the Terminal bell, but in this context, it terminates the escape sequence.)

Using AppleScript to Manipulate the Terminal

AppleScript is a powerful programming language used to automate Mac OS X applications. The Mac OS X Terminal is one such application. You can run AppleScript commands at the shell prompt using the *osascript* utility. The \ character tells the shell that you want to enter a single command on several lines (when you use this, the shell will prompt you with a ? character):

```
osascript -e \
'tell app "Terminal" to set option of first window to value'
```

For example, to minimize your current Terminal window:

```
$ osascript -e \
> 'tell app "Terminal" to set miniaturized of first window to true'
$
```

For a complete list of properties you can manipulate with AppleScript, open the Script Editor (*/Applications/AppleScript*) and select File → Open Dictionary. Open the Terminal dictionary and examine the properties available under *window*. If a property is marked [r/o], it is read-only, which means you can't modify it on the fly.

Working with .term Files

A quite useful capability of Terminal is the ability to create a specific Terminal window, customize its appearance and behavior, and then save that configuration as a *.term* file. Later, simply double-click on the *.term* file and you'll have your Terminal window back and ready to go, exactly as you set it up previously. Even better, you can set up multiple windows and have them all saved into a single *.term* file and then collectively relaunched when you restart the Terminal program.

As an example, we have set up the main Terminal window exactly as we prefer—large, blue text on a white background—and would like to save it as a *.term* file. To accomplish this, choose File → Save As. You'll be prompted with the dialog shown in Figure 1-12.

Perhaps the most interesting option is the checkbox "Open this file when Terminal starts up". Set things up the way you want and automatically, every time you start up Terminal, you could find a half dozen different size and different color windows on your desktop, all ready to go. Further, notice that instead of having a shell, you could have some start up running specific commands. A popular command to use is top or tail -f /var/log/system.log, to help keep an eye on how your system is performing. Explore the pop-up menu too; that's where you choose a single window to save as a *.term*, or specify "All Windows" to save them all in a single *.term* file.

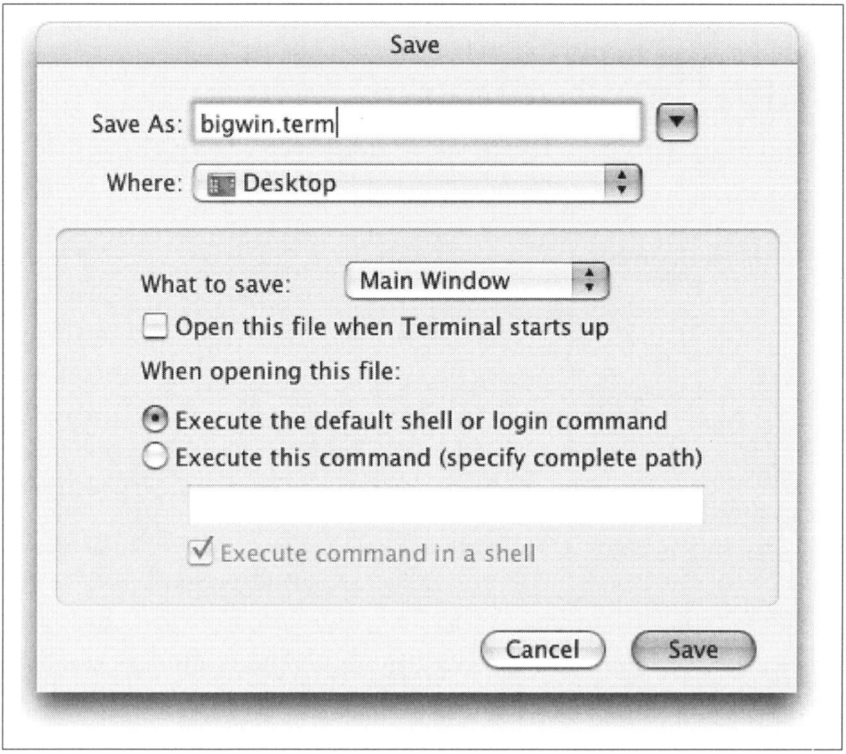

Figure 1-12. Saving a .term file

Further Customization

There's not much more you can do with the Terminal application than what's shown in this chapter, but there's an infinite amount of customization possible with the *bash* shell (or any other shell you might have picked). To learn more about how to customize your shell, read the manpage. Be warned, though, the *bash* manpage is over 4,500 lines long!

Oh, and in case you're wondering, manpages are the Unix version of online help documentation. Just about every command-line (Unix) command has a corresponding manpage with lots of information on starting flags, behaviors, and much more. You can access any manpage by simply typing **man** *cmd*. Start with **man man** to learn more about the man system.

For more information on customizing *bash*, see Cameron Newham and Bill Rosenblatts' book *Learning the bash Shell*, or *Unix Power Tools*, by Jerry Peek, Tim O'Reilly, and Mike Loukides, both available from O'Reilly.

## CHAPTER 2

Using the Terminal

With a typical Unix system, a staff person has to set up a Unix account for you before you can use it. With Mac OS X, however, the operating system installation automatically creates a default user account. The account is identified by your *username*, which is usually a single word or an abbreviation. Think of this account as your office—it's your personal place in the Unix environment.

When you log into your Mac OS X system, you're automatically logged into your Unix account as well. In fact, your Desktop and other customized features of your Mac OS X environment have corresponding features in the Unix environment. Your files and programs can be accessed either through the Mac Finder or through a variety of Unix command-line utilities that you can reach from within Mac OS X's Terminal window.

Working with the Terminal

To get into the Unix environment, launch the Terminal application (go to Finder → Applications → Utilities → Terminal). If you expect to use the Terminal a lot, drag the Terminal icon from the Finder window onto the Dock. You can then launch Terminal with a single click.) Once Terminal is running, you'll see a window like the one in Figure 2-1.

Once you have a window open and you're typing commands, it's helpful to know that regular Mac OS X copy and paste commands work, so it's simple to send an email message to a colleague showing your latest Unix interaction, or to paste some text from a web page into a file you're editing with a Unix text editor such as vi.

Figure 2-1. The Terminal window

You can also have a number of different Terminal windows open if that helps your workflow. Simply use ⌘–N to open each one, and ⌘–~ to cycle between them without removing your hands from the keyboard.

If you have material in your scroll buffer you want to find, use ⌘–F (or select Find → Find from the Edit menu) and enter the specific text. ⌘–G (Find → Next) lets you search down the scroll buffer for the next occurrence, and ⌘–D (Find → Previous) lets you search up the scroll buffer for the previous occurrence. You can also search for material by highlighting a passage, entering ⌘–E (Use → Selection for Find), or jumping to the selected material with ⌘–J (Jump to Selection). You can also save an entire Terminal session as a text file with File → Save Text As, and you can print the entire session with File → Print. It's a good idea to study the key sequences shown in the Scrollback menu, as illustrated in Figure 2-2.

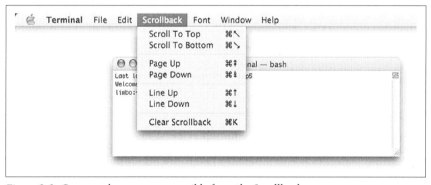

Figure 2-2. Command sequences accessible from the Scrollback menu

There are some symbols in the Scrollback menu you might not have seen before in your Mac OS X exploration: the upward facing diagonal arrow for Scroll to Top is the Top or Home key on your keyboard, and the downward facing diagonal arrow for Scroll to Bottom is the End key. You can move up a page with the Page Up key, and down a page with the Page Down key. To move up or down lines, use ⌘-Up Arrow or ⌘-Down Arrow, as needed.

Inside the Terminal window, you're working with a program called a *shell*. The shell interprets command lines you enter, runs programs you ask for, and generally coordinates what happens between you and the Unix operating system. The default shell on Mac OS X is called *bash* (it used to be *tcsh* in previous versions of Mac OS X). Other available shells include the Bourne shell (*sh*), the C shell (*csh*), the Tabbed C shell (*tcsh*), and the Z shell (*zsh*). A popular shell on other versions of Unix (not available by default on Mac OS X) is the Korn shell (*ksh*). To change the shell that Terminal uses, see "Launching Terminal" in Chapter 1.

For a beginner, differences between shells are slight. If you plan to work with Unix a lot, though, you should learn more about your shell and its special commands.

 To find out which shell you're using, run the command echo $SHELL. (See the section "Entering a Command" later in this chapter.) The answer, which will be something like */bin/ bash*, is your shell's pathname and name.

The Shell Prompt

When the system is ready to run a command, the shell outputs a *prompt* to tell you that you can enter a command.

The default prompt in *bash* is the computer name (which might be something automatically generated, such as dhcp-254-108, or a name you've given your system), the current directory (which might be represented by ~, Unix's shorthand for your home directory), your login name, and a dollar sign. For example, the complete prompt might look like this: limbo:~ taylor$. The prompt can be customized, though, so your own shell prompt may be different. We showed you how to customize your prompt in Chapter 1.

A prompt that ends with a hash mark (#) usually means you're logged in as the *superuser*. The superuser doesn't have the protections for standard users that are built into the Unix system. If you don't know Unix well, you can inadvertently damage your system software when you are logged in as the superuser. In this case, we recommend that you stop work until you've found out how to access your personal Unix account. The simplest solution is to open a new Terminal window (File → New Shell) and work in that window. If you've still got the superuser prompt, it means that you either logged into Mac OS X as the superuser or your shell prompt has been customized to end with a #, even when you're not the superuser. Try logging out of Mac OS X (File → Log Out) and logging back in as yourself.

Entering a Command

Entering a command line at the shell prompt tells the computer what to do. Each command line includes the name of a Unix program. When you press Return, the shell interprets your command line and executes the program.

The first word that you type at a shell prompt is always a Unix command (or program name). Like most things in Unix, program names are case sensitive; if the program name is lowercase (and most are), you must type it in lowercase. Some simple command lines have just one word, which is the program name. For more information, see the section "Syntax of a Unix Command Line" later in this chapter.

date

An example of a single-word command is date. Entering the command date displays the current date and time:

```
$ date
Tue Sep 23 12:57:06 MDT 2003
$
```

As you type a command line, the system simply collects your keyboard input. Pressing the Return key tells the shell that you've finished entering text, and it can run the program.

who

Another simple command is who. It displays a list of each logged-on user's username, terminal number, and login time. Try it now, if you'd like.

The who program can also tell you which account is currently using the Terminal application, in case you have multiple user accounts on your Mac. The command line for this is who am i. This command line consists of the command (who, the program's name) and arguments (am i). (Arguments are explained in the section "Syntax of Unix Command Lines" later in this chapter.) For example:

```
$ who am i
taylor    ttyp1    Sep 23 16:26
```

The response shown in this example says that:

- "taylor" is the username. The username is the same as the Short Name you define when you create a new user with System Preferences → Accounts → +.

- Terminal p1 is in use. This cryptic syntax, ttyp1, is a holdover from the early days of Unix. All you need to know as a Unix beginner is that each time you open a new terminal window, the number at the end of the name gets incremented. The first one is ttyp1, the second ttyp2, and so on. The terminal ID also appears in the titlebar of the Terminal window.

- A new Terminal window was opened at 4:26 in the afternoon of September 23rd.

Recalling Previous Commands

Modern Unix shells remember commands you've typed previously. They can even remember commands from previous login sessions. This handy feature can save you a lot of retyping of common commands. As with many things in Unix, though, there are several different ways to do this; we don't have room to show and explain them all. You can get more information from sources listed in Chapter 10.

After you've typed and executed several commands, try pressing the Up Arrow key on your keyboard. You will see the previous command after your shell prompt, just as you typed it before. Pressing the Up Arrow again recalls the previous command, and so on. Also, as you'd expect, the Down Arrow key will recall more recent commands.

To execute one of these remembered commands, just press the Return key. (Your cursor doesn't even have to be at the end of the command line.)

Once you've recalled a command, you can also edit it as necessary. If you don't want to execute any remembered commands, cancel the command shown with ⌘-. or Control-C. The next section explains both of these.

Correcting a Command

What if you make a mistake in a command line? Suppose you typed dare instead of date and pressed the Return key before you realized your mistake? The shell will give you an error message:

```
$ dare
-bash: dare: command not found
$
```

Don't be too concerned about getting error messages. Sometimes you'll get an error even if it appears that you typed the command correctly. This can be caused by accidentally typing control characters that are invisible on the screen. Once the prompt returns, reenter your command.

As we said earlier (in the section "Working with the Terminal"), you can recall previous commands and edit command lines. Use the Up-Arrow key to recall a previous command.

To edit the command line, use the Left-Arrow and Right-Arrow keys to move your cursor to the point where you want to make a change. You can use the Delete key to erase characters to the left of the cursor, and type in changes as needed.

If you have logged into your Macintosh remotely from another system (see Chapter 8), your keyboard may be different. The erase character differs between systems and accounts, and can be customized. The most common erase characters are:

- Delete or Del
- Control-H

Control-C or ⌘-. will interrupt or cancel a command, and can be used in many (but not all) cases when you want to quit what you're doing.

Other common control characters are:

Control-U
  Erases the whole input line; you can start over.

Control-S
  Pauses output from a program that's writing to the screen. This can be confusing; we don't recommend using Control-S but want you to be aware of it.

Control-Q
  Restarts output after a Control-S pause.

Control-D
  Signals the end of input for some programs (such as cat, explained in the section "Putting Text in a File" in Chapter 6) and returns you to a shell prompt. If you type Control-D at a shell prompt, it quits your shell. Depending on your preferences, your Terminal window either closes or sits there, which is useless, until you manually close the window.

Ending Your Session

To end a Unix session, you must exit the shell. You should *not* end a session just by quitting the Terminal application or closing the terminal window. It's possible that you might have started a process running in the background (see Chapter 7), and closing the window could therefore interrupt the process so it won't complete. Instead, type exit at a shell prompt.

The window will either close or simply not display any sort of prompt; you can then safely quit the Terminal application. If you've started a background process, you'll instead get one of the messages described in the next section.

Problem checklist

The first few times you use Mac OS X, you aren't likely to have the following problems. But you may encounter these problems later, as you do more advanced work.

You get another shell prompt, or the shell says "logout: not login shell".
> You've been using a subshell (a shell created by your original Terminal shell). To end each subshell, type exit (or just type Control-D) until the Terminal window closes.

The shell says "There are stopped jobs" or "There are running jobs".
> Mac OS X and many other Unix systems have a feature called *job control* that lets you suspend a program temporarily while it's running or keep it running separately in the "background." One or more programs you ran during your session has not ended but is stopped (paused) or in the background. Enter **fg** to bring each stopped job into the foreground, then quit the program normally. (See Chapter 9 for more information.)

The Terminal application refuses to quit, saying "Closing this window will terminate the following processes inside it:", followed by a list of programs.
> Terminal tries to help by not quitting when you're in the middle of running a command. Cancel the dialog box and make sure you don't have any commands running that you forgot about.

Syntax of a Unix Command Line

Unix command lines can be simple, one-word entries such as the date command. They can also be more complex; you may need to type more than the command or program name.*

A Unix command can have *arguments*. An argument can be an option or a filename. The general format for a Unix command line is:

```
command option(s) filename(s)
```

---

* The command can be the name of a Unix program (such as date), or it can be a command that's built into the shell (such as exit). You probably don't need to worry about this!

There isn't a single set of rules for writing Unix commands and arguments, but these general rules work in most cases:

- Enter commands in lowercase.

- *Options* modify the way in which a command works. Options are often single letters prefixed with a dash (-, also called "hyphen" or "minus") and set off by any number of spaces or tabs. Multiple options in one command line can be set off individually (such as -a -b). In most cases, you can combine them after a single dash (such as -ab), but most commands' documentation doesn't tell you whether this will work; you'll have to try it.

  Some commands also have options made from complete words or phrases and starting with two dashes, such as --delete or --confirm-delete. When you enter a command line, you can use this option style, the single-letter options (which each start with a single dash), or both.

- The argument *filename* is the name of a file you want to use. Most Unix programs also accept multiple filenames, separated by spaces or specified with wildcards (see Chapter 8). If you don't enter a filename correctly, you may get a response such as "*filename*: no such file or directory" or "*filename*: cannot open."

  Some commands, such as who (shown earlier in this chapter), have arguments that aren't filenames.

- You must type spaces between commands, options, and filenames. You'll need to "quote" filenames that contain spaces. For more information, see the section "File and Directory Names" in Chapter 4.

- Options come before filenames.

- In a few cases, an option has another argument associated with it; type this special argument just after its option. Most options don't work this way, but you should know about them. The sort command is an example of this feature: you can tell sort to write the sorted text to a filename given after its -o option. In the following example, sort reads the file *sortme* (given as an argument), and writes to the file *sorted* (given after the -o option):

      $ sort -o sorted -n sortme

  We also used the -n option in that example. But -n is a more standard option; it has nothing to do with the final argument sortme on that command line. So, we also could have written the command line this way:

      $ sort -n -o sorted sortme

  Don't be too concerned about these special cases, though. If a command needs an option like this, its documentation will say so.

- Command lines can have other special characters, some of which we see later in this book. They can also have several separate commands. For instance, you can write two or more commands on the same command line, each separated by a semicolon (;). Commands entered this way are executed one after another by the shell.

Mac OS X has a lot of commands! Don't try to memorize all of them. In fact, you'll probably need to know just a few commands and their options. As time goes on, you'll learn these commands and the best way to use them for your job. We cover some useful commands in later chapters. This book's quick reference card has quick reminders.

Let's look at a sample command. The ls program displays a list of files. You can use it with or without options and arguments. If you enter:

    $ ls

you'll see a list of filenames. But if you enter:

    $ ls -l

there will be an entire line of information for each file. The -l option (a dash and a lowercase letter "L") changes the normal ls output to a long format. You can also get information about a particular file by using its name as the second argument. For example, to find out about a file called *chap1*, enter:

    $ ls -l chap1

Many Unix commands have more than one option. For instance, ls has the -a (all) option for listing hidden files. You can use multiple options in either of these ways:

    $ ls -a -l
    $ ls -al

You must type one space between the command name and the dash that introduces the options. If you enter **ls-al**, the shell will say "ls-al: command not found."

Exercise: Entering a Few Commands

The best way to get used to the Terminal is to enter some commands. To run a command, type the command and then press the Return key. Remember that almost all Unix commands are typed in lowercase.

Here are a few to try:

Task	Command
Get today's date.	date
List logged-in users.	who

Task	Command
Obtain more information about users.	`who -u, finger,` or `w`
Find out who is at your terminal.	`who am i`
Enter two commands in the same line.	`who am i;date`
Mistype a command.	`woh`

In this session, you've tried several simple commands and seen the results on the screen.

Types of Commands

When you use a program, you'll want to know how to control it. How can you tell it what job you want done? Do you give instructions before the program starts, or after it's started? There are several general ways to give commands on a Mac OS X system. It's good to be aware of them.

Graphical programs

Some programs work only within the graphical window environment (on Mac OS X, this is called Aqua). On Mac OS X, you can run these programs using the open command. For instance, when you type **open -a Chess** at a shell prompt, the chess game starts. It opens one or more windows on your screen. The program has its own way to receive your commands—through menus and buttons on its windows, for instance. Although you can't interact with these programs using traditional Unix utilities, Mac OS X includes the *osascript* utility, which lets you run AppleScript commands from the Unix shell.

Noninteractive Unix programs

You saw in the section "Syntax of a Unix Command Line" that you can enter many Unix commands at a shell prompt. These programs work in a window system (from a Terminal window) or from any terminal. You control those programs from the Unix command line—that is, by typing options and arguments from a shell prompt before you start the program. After you start the program, wait for it to finish; you generally don't interact with it.

Interactive Unix programs

Some Unix programs that work in the terminal window have commands of their own. (If you'd like some examples, see Chapters 3 and 4.) These programs may accept options and arguments on their command lines. But, once you start a program, it prints its own prompt and/or menus, and it understands its own commands. It also takes instructions from your keyboard that weren't given on its command line.

For instance, if you enter **ftp** at a shell prompt, you'll see a new prompt from the ftp program. Enter FTP commands to transfer files to and from remote systems. When you enter the special command **quit** to quit the ftp program, ftp will stop prompting you. Then you'll get another shell prompt, where you can enter other Unix commands.

The Unresponsive Terminal

During your Unix session, your terminal may not respond when you type a command, or the display on your screen may stop at an unusual place. That's called a "hung" or "frozen" terminal or session. Note that most of the techniques in this section apply to a terminal window, but not to nonterminal windows such as a web browser.

A session can hang for several reasons. For instance, your computer can get too busy; the Terminal application has to wait its turn. In that case, your session resumes after a few moments. You should *not* try to "un-hang" the session by entering extra commands, because those commands will all take effect after Terminal comes back to life.

 If your display becomes garbled, press Control-L. In the shell, this will clear the screen and display the prompt. In a full-screen program, such as a text editor, it will redraw the screen.

If the system doesn't respond for quite a while (how long that is depends on your individual situation; ask other users about their experiences), the following solutions usually work. Try the following steps in the order shown until the system responds:

Press the Return key once.
> You may have typed text at a prompt (for example, a command line at a shell prompt) but haven't yet pressed Return to say that you're done typing and your text should be interpreted.

Try job control (see Chapter 7); type Control-Z.
> This control key sequence suspends a program that may be running and gives you a shell prompt. Now you can enter the jobs command to find the program's name, then restart the program with fg or terminate it with kill.

Press Control-C or ⌘–..

This interrupts a program that may be running. (Unless the program is run in the background; as described in the section, "Running a Command in the Background" in Chapter 7, the shell waits for a background program to finish before giving a new prompt. A long-running background program may thus appear to hang the terminal.) If this doesn't work the first time, try it once more; doing it more than twice usually won't help.

Type Control-Q.

If output has been stopped with Control-S, this will restart it. Note that some systems will automatically issue Control-S if they need to pause output; this character may not have been typed from the keyboard.

Type Control-D once at the beginning of a new line.

Some programs (such as `mail`) expect text from the user. A program may be waiting for an end-of-input character from you to tell it that you've finished entering text. Typing Control-D may cause you to log out, so you should try this only as a last resort.

Otherwise, close your Terminal window (⌘-W) and open a new one.

## CHAPTER 3

Using Unix

Once you launch Terminal, you can use the many facilities that Mac OS X provides. As a user, you have an account that gives you:

- A place in the filesystem where you can store your files
- A username that identifies you and lets you control access to your files
- An environment you can customize

The Mac OS X Filesystem

A *file* is the unit of storage in Mac OS X. A file can hold anything: text (a report you're writing, a to-do list), a program, digitally encoded pictures or sound, and so on. All of those are just sequences of raw data until they're interpreted by the right program.

Files are organized into directories (more commonly referred to as a *folder* on the Aqua (graphical) side of the Mac). A *directory* is actually a special kind of file where the system stores information about other files. You can think of a directory as a place, so that files are said to be contained *in* directories, and you work *inside* a directory. It's important that you realize that *everything is a file in Unix*. Whether you're working with a directory (perhaps moving files around) or editing a document, Unix fundamentally looks at everything as the same sort of container of information.

A *filesystem* includes all the files and directories on a mounted volume, such as your system's hard disk or your iDisk. This section introduces the Mac OS X filesystem. Later sections show how you can look in files and protect them. Chapter 4 has more information.

Your Home Directory

When you launch Terminal, you're placed in a directory called your *home directory*. This directory, which can also be opened in the Finder by clicking the Home icon, contains personal files, application preferences, and application data such as bookmarks. In your home directory, you can create your own files. As you'll see, you can also create directories within your home directory. Like folders in a file cabinet, this is a good way to organize your files.

Your Working Directory

Your *working directory* (also called your current directory) is the directory in which you're currently working. Every time you open a new Terminal window, your home directory is your working directory. When you change to another directory, the directory you move to becomes your working directory.

Unless you specify otherwise, all commands that you enter apply to the files in your working directory. In the same way, when you create files, they're created in your working directory unless you specify another directory. For instance, if you type the command **vi report**, the vi editor is started, and a file named *report* is created in your working directory. But if you type a command such as **vi /Users/john/Documents/report**, a *report* file is created in a different directory—without changing your working directory. You'll learn more about this when we cover pathnames later in this chapter.

If you have more than one Terminal window open, each shell has its own working directory. Changing the working directory in one shell doesn't affect other Terminal windows.

The Directory Tree

All directories on Mac OS X are organized into a hierarchical structure that you can imagine as a family tree. The parent directory of the tree (the directory that contains all other directories) is known as the *root directory* and is written as a forward slash (/). The root directory is what you see if you open a new Finder window, click the Computer icon, and then open your startup disk.

The root directory contains several other directories. Figure 3-1 shows a visual representation of the top of the Mac OS X filesystem tree: the root directory and some directories under the root.)

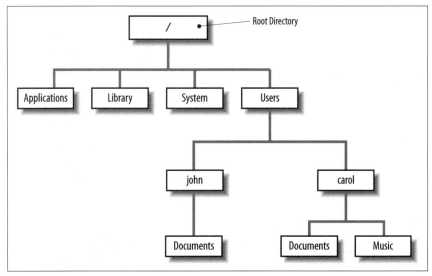

Figure 3-1. Example of a directory tree

Applications, *Library*, *System*, and *Users* are some of the *subdirectories* (child directories) of the root directory. There are several other directories that are invisible in the Finder but visible at the shell prompt (you can see them if you use the command ls /). These subdirectories are standard Unix directories: *bin*, *dev*, *etc*, *sbin*, *tmp*, *usr*, and *var*; they contain Unix system files. For instance, *bin* contains many Unix programs.

In our example, the parent directory of *Users* (one level above) is the root directory. *Users* has two subdirectories (one level below), *john* and *carol*. On a Mac OS X system, each directory has only one parent directory, but it may have one or more subdirectories.*

A subdirectory (such as *carol*) can have its own subdirectories (such as *Documents* and *Music*).

To specify a file or directory location, write its *pathname*. A pathname is like the address of the directory or file in the filesystem. We will look at pathnames in the next section.

On a basic Mac OS X system, all files in the filesystem are stored on disks connected to your computer. Mac OS X has a way to access files on other computers: a *networked filesystem*. Networked filesystems make a remote computer's files appear as if they're part of your computer's directory tree. For instance, when you mount your iDisk (Choose Go → iDisk → My iDisk

---

* The root directory at the top of the tree is *its own* parent.

in the Finder), Mac OS X mounts your iDisk on your desktop and also makes it available as a directory under */Volumes*. You can also mount shared directories from other Macintoshes or Windows machines (choose Go → Connect to Server... in the Finder). These will also appear in the */Volumes* directory, as will other disks, such as external FireWire drives.

Absolute Pathnames

As you saw earlier, the Unix filesystem organizes its files and directories in an inverted tree structure with the root directory at the top. An *absolute pathname* tells you the path of directories through which you must travel to get from the root to the directory or file you want. In a pathname, put slashes (/) between the directory names.

For example, */Users/john* is an absolute pathname. It identifies one (*only* one!) directory. Here's how:

- The root is the first slash (/).
- The directory *Users* (a subdirectory of *root*) is second.
- The directory *john* (a subdirectory of *Users*) is last.

 Be sure that you do not type spaces anywhere in the pathname. If there are spaces in one or more of the directories, you need to either quote the entire directory pathname, or preface each space with a backslash to ensure that the shell understands that the spaces are part of the pathname itself.

Figure 3-2 shows this structure.

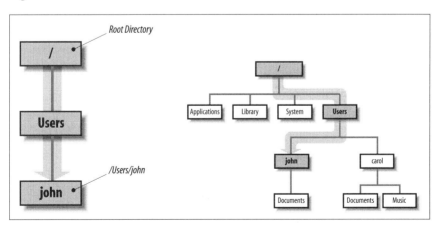

Figure 3-2. Absolute path of directory john

In Figure 3-2, you'll see that the directory *john* has a subdirectory named *Documents*. Its absolute pathname is */Users/john/Documents*.

The root is always indicated by the slash (/) at the start of the pathname. In other words, an absolute pathname always starts with a slash.

Relative Pathnames

You can also locate a file or directory with a *relative pathname*. A relative pathname gives the location relative to your working directory.

Unless you use an absolute pathname (starting with a slash), Unix assumes that you're using a relative pathname. Like absolute pathnames, relative pathnames can go through more than one directory level by naming the directories along the path.

For example, if you're currently in the *Users* directory (see Figure 3-2), the relative pathname to the *carol* directory below is simply *carol*. The relative pathname to the *Music* directory below that is *carol/Music*.

Notice that neither pathname in the previous paragraph starts with a slash. That's what makes them relative pathnames! Relative pathnames start at the working directory, not the root directory. In other words, a relative pathname never starts with a slash.

Pathname puzzle

Here's a short but important question. The previous example explains the relative pathname *carol/Music*. What do you think Unix would say about the pathname */carol/Music*? (Look again at Figure 3-2.)

Unix would say "No such file or directory." Why? (Please think about that before you read more. It's very important and it's one of the most common beginner's mistakes.) Here's the answer. Because it starts with a slash, the pathname */carol/Music* is an absolute pathname that starts from the root. It says to look in the root directory for a subdirectory named *carol*. But there is no subdirectory named *carol* one level directly below the root, so the pathname is wrong. The only absolute pathname to the *Music* directory is */Users/carol/Music*.

Relative pathnames up

You can go up the tree with the shorthand .. (dot dot) for the parent directory. As you saw earlier, you can also go down the tree by using subdirectory names. In either case (up or down), separate each level by a / (slash).

Figure 3-3 shows part of Figure 3-1. If your working directory in the figure is *Documents*, then there are two pathnames for the *Music* subdirectory of *carol*. You already know how to write the absolute pathname, */Users/carol/Music*. You can also go up one level (with ..) to *carol*, then go down the tree to *Music*. Figure 3-3 illustrates this.

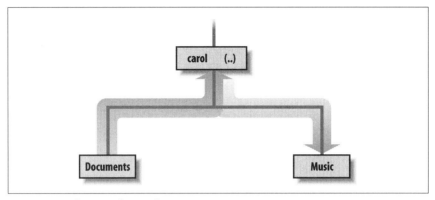

Figure 3-3. Relative pathname from Documents to Music

The relative pathname would be *../Music*. It would be wrong to give the relative address as *carol/Music*. Using *carol/Music* would say that *carol* is a subdirectory of your working directory instead of what it is in this case: the parent directory.

Absolute and relative pathnames are interchangeable. Unix programs simply follow whichever path you specify to wherever it leads. If you use an absolute pathname, the path starts from the root. If you use a relative pathname, the path starts from your current working directory. Choose whichever is easier at the moment.

Changing Your Working Directory

Once you know the absolute or relative pathname of a directory where you'd like to work, you can move up and down the Mac OS X filesystem to reach it. The following sections explain some helpful commands for navigating through a directory tree.

pwd

To find which directory you're currently in, use pwd (print working directory), which prints the absolute pathname of your working directory. The pwd command takes no arguments:

```
$ pwd
/Users/john
$
```

cd

You can change your working directory to any directory (including another user's directory, if you have permission) with the cd (change directory) command, which has the form:

> cd *pathname*

The argument is an absolute or a relative pathname (whichever is easier) for the directory you want to change to:

```
$ cd /Users/carol
$ pwd
/Users/carol
$ cd Documents
$ pwd
/Users/carol/Documents
$
```

 The command cd, with no arguments, takes you to your home directory from wherever you are in the filesystem.

Note that you can only change to another directory. You cannot cd to a filename. If you try, your shell (in this example, *bash*) gives you an error message:

```
$ cd /etc/manpath.config
-bash: cd: /etc/manpath.config:  Not a directory.
$
```

/etc/manpath.config is a file with information about the configuration of the man command.

One neat trick worth mentioning is that you can always have Terminal enter the path directly by dragging a file or folder icon from the Finder onto the active Terminal window.

Files in the Directory Tree

A directory can hold subdirectories. And, of course, a directory can hold files. Figure 3-4 is a close-up of the filesystem around *john*'s home directory. There are six directories shown, along with the *mac-rocks* file created by using the touch command, as demonstrated in the sidebar "Two Ways to Explore Your Filesystem."

Pathnames to files are made the same way as pathnames to directories. As with directories, files' pathnames can be absolute (starting from the root directory) or relative (starting from the working directory). For example, if

Two Ways to Explore Your Filesystem

Every file and folder that you view from the Finder is also accessible from the Unix shell. Changes made in one environment are reflected (almost) immediately in the other. For example, the Desktop folder is also the Unix directory */Users/yourname/Desktop*.

Just for fun, open a Finder window, move to your *Home* folder, and keep it visible while you type these commands at the shell prompt:

```
$ cd
$ touch mac-rocks
```

Switch back to the Finder (you can click on the desktop) and watch a file called *mac-rocks* appear magically. (The touch command creates an empty file with the name you specify.)

Now type:

```
$ rm mac-rocks
```

Return to the Finder, and watch the file disappear. The rm command removes the file.

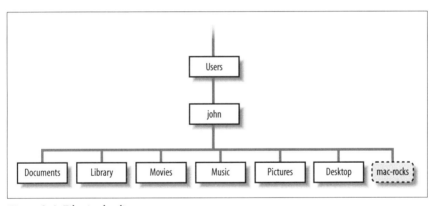

Figure 3-4. Files in the directory tree

your working directory is *Users*, the relative pathname to the *Documents* directory below would be *john/Documents*. The relative pathname to the *mac-rocks* file would be *john/mac-rocks*.

Unix filesystems can hold things that aren't directories or files, such as symbolic links (similar to aliases), devices (the */dev* directory contains entries for devices attached to the system), and sockets (network communication channels). You may see some of them as you explore the filesystem. We don't cover those advanced topics in this little book.

Listing Files with ls

To use the `cd` command, you must know which entries in a directory are subdirectories and which are files. The `ls` command lists entries in the directory tree and can also show you which is which.

When you enter the `ls` command, you get a list of the files and subdirectories contained in your working directory. The syntax is:

```
ls option(s) directory-and-filename(s)
```

If you've just moved into an empty directory, entering `ls` without any arguments may seem to do nothing. This isn't surprising, because you haven't made any files in your working directory. If you have no files, nothing is displayed; you'll simply get a new shell prompt:

```
$ ls
$
```

But if you're in your home directory, `ls` displays the names of the files and directories in that directory. The output depends on what's in your directory. The screen should look something like this:

```
$ ls
Desktop        Library        Music          Public         mac-rocks
Documents      Movies         Pictures       Sites
$
```

Sometimes `ls` might display filenames in a single column. If yours does, you can make a multicolumn display with the `-C` option or the `-x` option. `ls` has a lot of options that change the information and display format.

The `-a` option (for all) is guaranteed to show you some more files, as in the following example:

```
$ ls -a
.                    .Trash          Library         Public
..                   .bash_history   Movies          Sites
.CFUserTextEncoding  Desktop         Music           mac-rocks
.DS_Store            Documents       Pictures
$
```

When you use `ls -a`, you'll always see at least two entries with the names `.` (dot) and `..` (dot dot). As mentioned earlier, `..` is always the relative pathname to the parent directory. A single `.` always stands for its working directory; this is useful with commands such as `cp` (see the section "Copying Files" in Chapter 4). There may also be other files, such as *.bashrc* or *.Trash*. Any entry whose name begins with a dot is hidden—it's listed only if you use `ls -a`.

To get more information about each item that `ls` lists, add the `-l` option. (That's a lowercase "L" for "long.") This option can be used alone, or in combination with -a, as shown in Figure 3-5. Because *.bash_history* and *.Trash* are hidden files, only *ch1* and *ch2* would appear if you viewed this directory in the Finder.

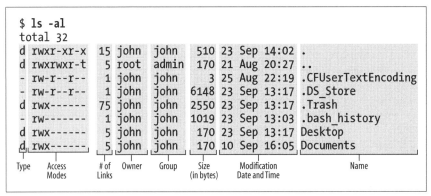

Figure 3-5. Output from ls –al

The long format provides the following information about each item:

Total n
States the amount of storage (*n*) used by everything in this directory. (This is measured in *blocks*.) On Mac OS X, blocks are 1,024 bytes in size.

Type
Tells whether the item is a directory (d) or a plain file (-). (There are other less common types as well.)

Access modes
Specifies three types of users (yourself, your group, and all others) who are allowed to read (r), write (w), or execute (x) your files or directories. We'll talk more about access modes later.

Links
Lists the number of files or directories linked to this directory. (This isn't the same as a web page link.)

Owner
States the user who created or owns this file or directory.

Group
Lists the group that owns the file or directory.

Size (in bytes)
States the size of the file or directory. (A directory is actually a special type of file. Here, the "size" of a directory is of the directory file itself, not the total of all the files in that directory.)

Modification date

States the date when the file was last modified or when the directory contents last changed (when something in the directory was added, renamed, or removed). If an entry was modified more than six months ago, ls shows the year instead of the time.

Name

Tells the name of the file or directory.

Notice especially the columns that list the owner and group of the files, and the access modes (also called permissions). The person who creates a file is its owner; if you've created any files, this column should show your username. You also belong to a group. Files you create are marked either with the name of your group or, in some cases, the group that owns the directory.

The permissions show who can read, write, or execute the file or directory. The permissions have 10 characters. The first character shows the file type (d for directory or - for a plain file). The other characters come in groups of 3. The first group, characters 2–4, shows the permissions for the file's owner (which is you if you created the file). The second group, characters 5–7, shows permissions for other members of the file's group. The third group, characters 8–10, shows permissions for all other users.

For example, the permissions for *.DS_Store* in Figure 3-5 are -rw-r--r--. The first hyphen, -, indicates that it's a plain file. The next three characters, rw-, mean that the owner, *john*, has both read (r) and write (w) permissions. The next two sets of permissions are both r--, which means that other users who belong to the file's group *john*, as well as all other users of the system, can only read the file; they don't have write permission, so they can't change what's in the file. No one has execute (x) permission, which should be used only for executable files (programs) and directories.

In the case of directories, x means the permission to access the directory— for example, to run a command that reads a file there or to use a subdirectory. Notice that the first directory shown in Figure 3-5, *Desktop*, is executable (accessible) by *john*, but completely closed off to everyone else on the system. A directory with write (w) permission allows deleting, renaming, or adding files within the directory. Read (r) permission allows listing the directory with ls.

You can use the chmod command to change the permissions of your files and directories (see the section "Protecting and Sharing Files" later in this chapter).

If you need to know only which files are directories and which are executable files, you can use the -F option with ls. If you give the pathname to a directory, ls lists the directory but does *not* change your working directory. The pwd command here shows this:

```
$ ls -F /Users/andy
$ ls -F
Desktop/        Library/        Music/        Public/        mac-rocks
Documents/      Movies/         Pictures/     Sites/
$ pwd
/Applications
$
```

ls -F puts a / (slash) at the end of each directory name. (The directory name doesn't really have a slash in it; that's just the shorthand ls -F uses to identify a directory.) In our example, every entry other than "mac-rocks" is a directory.. You can verify this by using ls -l and noting the d in the first field of the output. Files with an execute status (x), such as programs, are marked with an * (asterisk).

ls -R (recursive) lists a directory and all its subdirectories. This can make a very long list—especially when you list a directory near the root! (Piping the output of ls to a pager program solves this problem. There's an example in the section "Piping to a Pager" in Chapter 6.) You can combine other options with -R; for instance, ls -RF marks each directory and file type, while recursively listing files and directories.

Calculating File Size

You can find the size of a file with the du command:

```
$ du Documents/Outline.doc
300      Documents/Outline.doc
```

The size is reported in kilobytes, so *Outline.doc* is 300 KB in size. If you give du the name of a directory, it will calculate the sizes of everything in it:

```
$ du Library
8        Library/Application Support/AddressBook/Images
120      Library/Application Support/AddressBook
3776     Library/Application Support/Chess
...
```

If you want the total for the directory, use -s (summarize):

```
$ du -s Library
56120  Library
```

If you'd like separate totals for all directories and files, including hidden ones, use a wildcard pattern that ignores the . (current) and .. (parent) directories (see "Relative pathnames up," earlier in this chapter):

```
$ du -s * .[^.]*
40       Desktop
```

```
2200    Documents
56120   Library
...
438048  .Trash
8       .bash_history
```

You can also calculate your system's free disk space with df -h (the -h produces more user-friendly output):

```
$ df -h
Filesystem              Size  Used  Avail Capacity  Mounted on
/dev/disk2s10           7.3G  3.5G  3.7G    49%     /
devfs                   105K  105K   0B    100%     /dev
fdesc                   1.0K  1.0K   0B    100%     /dev
<volfs>                 512K  512K   0B    100%     /.vol
/dev/disk1s9             37G   17G   21G    45%     /Volumes/X
automount -nsl [273]     0B    0B    0B    100%     /Network
automount -fstab [290]   0B    0B    0B    100%     /automount/Servers
automount -static [290]  0B    0B    0B    100%     /automount/static
```

The first column (Filesystem) shows the Unix device name for the volume. The second column (Size) shows the total disk size, and it's followed by the amount of disk space used up (Used) and the amount that's available (Avail). After that, the Use% column shows the percentage of disk space used, followed by where the volume is mounted (Mounted on).

/ is the root of your filesystem (a volume that is named Macintosh HD by default). /dev contains files that correspond to hardware devices, and /.vol exposes some internals of the Mac OS X filesystem called *HFS+ file ids*. The last entry is a volume called Mac OS 9.

Completing File and Directory Names

Most Unix shells can complete a partly typed file or directory name for you. Different shells have different methods. If you're using the default shell in Mac OS X (i.e., *bash*), just type the first few letters of the name, then press Tab. If the shell can find just one way to finish the name, it will; your cursor will move to the end of the new name, where you can type more or press Return to run the command. (You can also edit or erase the completed name.)

What happens if more than one file or directory name matches what you've typed so far? The shell will beep at you to tell you that it couldn't find a unique match. To get a list of all possible completions, simply press the Tab key again and you will see a list of all names starting with the characters you've typed so far (you won't see anything if there are no matches). Here's an example from the *bash* shell:

```
$ cd /usr/bin
$ ma<Tab><Tab>
mach_init   machine   mail      mailq     mailstat  makedbm  makeinfo
man         manpath
$ ma
```

At this point, you could type another character or two—an i, for example—and then press Tab once more to list only the mail-related commands.

Multiple Commands on the Command Line

An extremely helpful technique for working with the Unix system is the ability to have more than one command specified on a single command line. Perhaps you want to run a command and find out how long it took to complete. This can be done by calling date before and after the command. If you hunt and peck out date each time, the timing is hardly going to be accurate. Much better is to put all three commands on the same line:

```
$ cd ; date ; du -s . ; date
Tue Sep 23 14:36:42 MDT 2003
4396680  .
Tue Sep 23 14:36:57 MDT 2003
```

This shows 4 different commands all strung together on a single command line. First, cd moves you into your home directory, then date shows the current date and time. The du -s command figures out how much disk space is used by the . (current) directory, and a second date command shows the time after the du command has run. Now you know it takes exactly 15 seconds to calculate disk space used by your home directory, rather than knowing it takes 25 seconds for you to type the command, for du to run, and for you to type date again.

Exercise: Exploring the Filesystem

You're now equipped to explore the filesystem with cd, ls, and pwd. Take a tour of the directory system, hopping one or many levels at a time, with a mixture of cd and pwd commands.

Task	Command
Go to your home directory.	cd
Find your working directory.	pwd
Change to new working directory with its absolute pathname.	cd /bin
List files in new working directory.	ls
Change directory to root and list it in one step. (Use the command separator: a semicolon.)	cd /; ls
Find your working directory.	pwd

Task	Command
Change to a subdirectory; use its relative pathname.	cd usr
Find your working directory.	pwd
Change to a subdirectory.	cd lib
Find your working directory.	pwd
Give a wrong pathname.	cd xqk
List files in another directory.	ls /bin
Find your working directory (notice that ls didn't change it).	pwd
Return to your home directory.	cd

Looking Inside Files with less

By now, you're probably tired of looking at files from the outside. It's like visiting a bookstore and looking at the covers, but never getting to open the book and read what's inside. Let's look at a program for reading text files.

If you want to "read" a long plain text file on the screen, you can use the less command to display one "page" (a Terminal window filled from top to bottom) of text at a time.

If you don't like less, you can try a very similar program named more. In fact, the name less is a play on the name of more, which came first (but less has more features than more). The syntax for less is:

```
less option(s) file(s)
```

less lets you move forward or backward in the files by any number of pages or lines; you can also move back and forth between two or more files specified on the command line. When you invoke less, the first "page" of the file appears. A prompt appears at the bottom of the Terminal window, as in the following example:

```
$ less ch03
A file is the unit of storage in Unix, as in most other systems.
A file can hold anything: text (a report you're writing,
   .
   .
   .
:
```

The basic less prompt is a colon (:); although, for the first screenful, less displays the file's name as a prompt. The cursor sits to the right of this prompt as a signal for you to enter a less command to tell less what to do. To quit, type q.

Like almost everything about less, the prompt can be customized. For example, using the -M starting flag on the less command line makes the prompt show the filename and your position in the file (as a percentage).

 If you want this to happen every time you use less, you can set the LESS environment variable to M (without a dash) in your shell setup file. See the section "Customizing Your Shell Environment" in Chapter 1.

You can set or unset most options temporarily from the less prompt. For instance, if you have the short less prompt (a colon), you can enter -M while less is running. less responds "Long prompt (press Return)," and for the rest of the session, less prompts with the filename, line number, and percentage of the file viewed.

To display the less commands and options available on your system, press h (for "help") while less is running. Table 3-1 lists some simple (but still quite useful) commands.

Table 3-1. Useful less commands

Command	Description	Command	Description
SPACE	Display next page	v	Starts the vi editor
Return	Display next line	Control-L	Redisplay current page
*n*f	Move forward *n* lines	h	Help
b	Move backward one page	:n	Go to next file on command line
*n*b	Move backward *n* lines	:p	Go back to previous file on command line
/*word*	Search forward for *word*	q	Quit less
?*word*	Search backward for *word*		

Protecting and Sharing Files

Mac OS X makes it easy for users on the same system to share files and directories. For instance, everyone in a group can read documents stored in one of their manager's directories without needing to make their own copies, if the manager has allowed access. There might be no need to fill peoples' email inboxes with file attachments if everyone can access those files directly through the Unix filesystem.

Here's a brief introduction to file security and sharing. If you have critical security needs, or you just want more information, talk to your system staff or see an up-to-date book on Unix security such as *Practical Unix and Internet Security*, by Simson Garfinkel, Gene Spafford, and Alan Schwartz (O'Reilly).

Note that any admin user can use the sudo command (see "Superuser Privileges with sudo," later in this chapter) to do anything to any file at any time, no matter what its permissions are. So, access permissions won't keep your private information safe from *everyone*—although let's hope that you can trust the other folks who share your Macintosh!

Directory Access Permissions

A directory's access permissions help to control access to the files and subdirectories in that directory:

- If a directory has read permission, a user can run ls to see what's in the directory and use wildcards to match files in it.
- A directory that has write permission allows users to add, rename, and delete files in the directory.
- To access a directory (that is, to read or write the files in the directory or to run the files if they're programs), a user needs execute permission on that directory. Note that to access a directory, a user must *also* have execute permission to all its parent directories, all the way up to the root.

Mac OS X includes a shared directory for all users: */Users/ Shared.* You can create files in this directory and modify files you have put there. However, you cannot modify a file there that's owned by another user.

File Access Permissions

The access permissions on a file control what can be done to the file's *contents.* The access permissions on the directory where the file is kept control whether the file can be renamed or removed. If this seems confusing, think of it this way: the directory is actually a list of files. Adding, renaming, or removing a file changes the contents of the directory. If the directory isn't writable, you can't change that list.

Read permission controls whether you can read a file's contents. Write permission lets you change a file's contents. A file shouldn't have execute permission unless it's a program or a script.

Setting Permissions with chmod

Once you know what permissions a file or directory needs—and if you're the owner (listed in the third column of ls -l output)—you can change the permissions with the chmod program. If you select a file or directory in the

---

Finder, and then choose File → Get Info (⌘-I), you can also change the permissions using the Ownership & Permissions section of the Get Info dialog (see Figure 3-6).

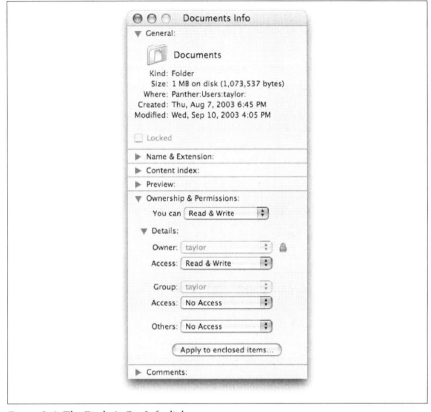

Figure 3-6. The Finder's Get Info dialog

There are two ways to change permissions: by specifying the permissions to add or delete, or by specifying the exact permissions. For instance, if a directory's permissions are almost correct, but you also need to make it writable by its group, tell chmod to add group-write permission. But if you need to make more than one change to the permissions—for instance, if you want to add read and execute permission but delete write permission—it's easier to set all permissions explicitly instead of changing them one by one. The syntax is:

```
chmod permissions file(s)
```

Let's start with the rules; we see examples next. The *permissions* argument has three parts, which you must give in order with no space between.

1. The category of permission you want to change. There are three: the owner's permission (which `chmod` calls "user," abbreviated `u`), the group's permission (`g`), or others' permission (`o`). To change more than one category, string the letters together, such as `go` for "group and others," or simply use `a` to mean "all" (same as `ugo`).

2. Whether you want to add (`+`) the permission, delete (`-`) it, or specify it exactly (`=`).

3. What permissions you want to affect: read (`r`), write (`w`), or execute (`x`). To change more than one permission, string the letters together—for example, `rw` for "read and write."

Some examples should make this clearer! In the following command lines, you can replace *dirname* or *filename* with the pathname (absolute or relative) of the directory or file. An easy way to change permissions on the working directory is by using its relative pathname, . (dot), as in `chmod o- w .`. You can combine two permission changes in the same `chmod` command by separating them with a comma (`,`), as shown in the final example.

- To protect a file from accidental editing, delete everyone's write permission with the command:

    ```
    chmod a-w filename
    ```

    On the other hand, if you own an unwritable file that you want to edit, but you don't want to change other peoples' write permissions, you can add "user" (owner) write permission with:

    ```
    chmod u+w filename
    ```

- To keep yourself from accidentally removing files (or adding or renaming files) in an important directory of yours, delete your own write permission with the command:

    ```
    chmod u-w dirname
    ```

    If other users have that permission too, you could delete everyone's write permission with:

    ```
    chmod a-w dirname
    ```

- If you want you and your group to be able to read and write all the files in your working directory—but those files have various permissions now, so adding and deleting the permissions individually would be a pain—this is a good place to use the `=` operator to set the exact permissions you want. Use the filename wildcard `*`, which means "everything in this directory" (explained in the section "File and Directory Wildcards" in Chapter 4) and type:

    ```
    chmod ug=rw *
    ```

- If your working directory has any subdirectories, though, that command would be wrong because it takes away execute permission from the subdirectories, so the subdirectories couldn't be accessed anymore. In that case, you could try a more specific wildcard. Or, instead of a wildcard, you can simply list the filenames you want to change, separated by spaces, as in:

  ```
  chmod ug=rw afile bfile cfile
  ```

- To protect the files in a directory and all its subdirectories from everyone else on your system, but still keep the access permissions *you* have there, you could use:

  ```
  chmod go-rwx dirname
  ```

  to delete all "group" and "others" permission to read, write, and execute. A simpler way is to use the command:

  ```
  chmod go= dirname
  ```

  to set "group" and "others" permission to exactly nothing.

- You want full access to a directory. Other people on the system should be able to see what's in the directory (and read or edit the files if the file permissions allow it) but not rename, remove, or add files. To do that, give yourself all permissions, but give "group" and "others" only read and execute permission. Use the command:

  ```
  chmod u=rwx,go=rx dirname
  ```

After you change permissions, it's a good idea to check your work with `ls -l` *filename* or `ls -ld` *dirname*. (Without the -d option, `ls` will list the contents of the directory instead of its permissions and other information.)

Problem checklist

I get the message "chmod: Not owner".

Only the owner of a file or directory (or the superuser) can set its permissions. Use `ls -l` to find the owner or use superuser privileges (see "Superuser Privileges with sudo," later in this chapter).

A file is writable, but my program says it can't be written.

First, check the file permissions with `ls -l` and be sure you're in the category (user, group, or others) that has write permission.

The problem may also be in the permissions of the file's directory. Some programs need permission to write more files into the same directory (for example, temporary files) or to rename files (for instance, making a file into a backup) while editing. If it's safe to add write permission to the directory (if other files in the directory don't need protection from removal or renaming), try that. Otherwise, copy the file to a writable directory (with cp), edit it there, then copy it back to the original directory.

Changing Group and Owner

Group ownership lets a certain group of users have access to a file or directory. You might need to let a different group have access. The chgrp program sets the group owner of a file or directory. You can set the group to any of the groups to which you belong. Because you're likely going to be administering your system, you can control the list of groups you're in. (In some situations, the system administrator controls the list of groups you're in.) The groups program lists your groups.

For example, if you're a designer creating a directory named *images* for several illustrators, the directory's original group owner might be *admin*. You'd like the illustrators, all of whom are in the group named *staff*, to access the directory; members of other groups should have no access. Use commands such as:

```
$ groups
gareth admin
$ mkdir images
$ ls -ld images
drwxr-xr-x   2 gareth  admin        68 Nov  6 09:53 images
$ chgrp staff images
$ chmod o= images
$ ls -ld images
drwxr-x---   2 gareth  staff        68 Nov  6 09:53 images
```

 Mac OS X also lets you set a directory's group ownership so that any files you later create in that directory will be owned by the same group as the directory. Try the command chmod g+s *dirname*. The permissions listing from ls -ld will now show an *s* in place of the second x, such as drwxr- s---.

The chown program changes the owner of a file or directory. Only the superuser can use chown (see "Superuser Privileges with sudo," later in this chapter).[*]

```
$ chown eric images
chown: changing ownership of `images': Operation not permitted
$ sudo chown eric images
Password:
$
```

---

[*] If you have permission to read another user's file, you can make a copy of it (with cp; see the section "Copying Files" in Chapter 4). You'll own the copy.

Changing Your Password

The ownership and permissions system described in this chapter depends on the security of your username and password. If others get your username and password, they can log into your account and do anything you can. They can read private information, corrupt or delete important files, send email messages as if they came from you, and more. If your computer is connected to a network, whether it be the Internet or a local network inside your organization, intruders may also be able to log in without sitting at your keyboard! See the section "Remote Logins" in Chapter 8 for one way this can be done.

Anyone may be able to get your username—it's usually part of your email address, for instance, or shows up as a file's owner in a long directory listing. Your password is what keeps others from logging in as you. Don't leave your password anywhere around your computer. Don't give your password to anyone who asks you for it unless you're sure he'll preserve your account security. Also, don't send your password by email; it can be stored, unprotected, on other systems and on backup tapes, where other people may find it and then break into your account.

If you think that someone knows your password, you should probably change it right away—although if you suspect that a computer "cracker" (or "hacker") is using your account to break into your system, you should ask your system administrator for advice first, if possible. You should also change your password periodically. Every few months is recommended.

A password should be easy for you to remember but hard for other people (or password-guessing programs) to guess. Here are some guidelines. A password should be between six and eight characters long. It should not be a word in any language, a proper name, your phone number, your address, or anything anyone else might know or guess that you'd use as a password. It's best to mix upper- and lowercase letters, punctuation, and numbers. A good way to come up with a unique but memorable password is to think of a phrase that only you might know, and use the first letters of each word (and punctuation) to create the password. For example, consider the password mlwsiF! ("My laptop was stolen in Florence!").

To change your password, you can use → System Preferences → Accounts, but you can also change it from the command line using the `passwd` command. After you enter the command, it prompts you to enter your old password. If the password is correct, it asks you to enter the new password—twice, to be sure there is no typing mistake.

```
$ passwd
Changing password for taylor.
```

```
Old password:
New password:
Retype new password:
```

For security, neither the old nor the new passwords appear as you type them.

Superuser Privileges with sudo

Your Mac OS X user account runs with restricted privileges; there are parts of the filesystem to which you don't have access, and there are certain activities that are prohibited until you supply a password. For example, when you run the Software Update utility from System Preferences, Mac OS X may ask you for your password before it proceeds. This extra authentication step allows Software Update to run installers with superuser privileges.

You can invoke these same privileges at the command line by prefixing a command with *sudo*, a utility that prompts you for your password and executes the command as the superuser. You must be an Admin user to use *sudo*. The user you created when you first set up your Mac will be an Admin user. You can add new Admin users or grant Admin status to a user in System Preferences → Accounts.

 What if you don't know your administrative password? If you forgot your password, read the Mac OS Help to direct you. You might need to reboot your computer off your original Mac OS X install CD-ROM, then when you get to the installer, select the Reset Password... option from the Installer menu. The program will then prompt you for a new password and set it for your machine. Reboot again (without the CD-ROM), and you should be set forever.

You may need to use *sudo* when you install Unix utilities or if you want to modify a file you don't own. Suppose that you accidentally created a file in the */Users* directory while you were doing something else as the superuser. You won't be able to modify it with your normal privileges, so you'll need to use *sudo*:

```
$ ls -l logfile.out
-rw-r--r--  1 root     wheel     1784064 Nov  6 11:25 logfile.out
$ rm logfile.out
override rw-r--r--  root/wheel for logfile.out? y
rm: logfile.out: Permission denied
$ sudo rm logfile.out
Password:
$ ls -l logfile.out
ls: logfile.out: No such file or directory
```

If you use *sudo* again within five minutes, it won't ask for your password. Be careful using *sudo*, since it gives you the ability to modify protected files, all of which are protected to ensure the system runs properly.

Exploring External Volumes

Earlier we mentioned that additional hard disks on your system and any network-based disks are all mounted onto the filesystem in the */Volumes* directory. Let's take a closer look to see how it works:

```
$ ls /Volumes
110GB           Extra 30        Panther         X
$ ls -l /Volumes
total 8
drwxrwxrwx  29 taylor  staff      986 22 Sep 16:37 110GB
drwxrwxrwx  11 taylor  unknown    374  4 Sep 23:28 Extra 30
lrwxr-xr-x   1 root    admin        1 23 Sep 12:30 Panther -> /
drwxrwxr-t  61 root    admin     2074 22 Sep 16:51 X
```

There are four disks available, one of which is actually the root (or boot) disk: Panther. Notice that the entry for Panther is different than the others, with the first character shown an l rather than a d. This means it's a link (see "Working with Links" in Chapter 4), which is confirmed by the fact that it's shown as Panther in the regular ls output, while the value of the alias is shown in the long listing (you can see that Panther actually points to /).

If you insert a CD or DVD into the system, it will also show up as a */Volumes* entry:

```
$ ls -l /Volumes
total 12
drwxrwxrwx  29 taylor   staff      986 22 Sep 16:37 110GB
dr-xr-xr-x   4 unknown  nogroup    136 17 Aug  2001 CITIZEN_KANE
drwxrwxrwx  11 taylor   unknown    374  4 Sep 23:28 Extra 30
lrwxr-xr-x   1 root     admin        1 23 Sep 12:30 Panther -> /
drwxrwxr-t  61 root     admin     2074 22 Sep 16:51 X
```

Plugging in an iPod and a digital camera proceeds as follows:

```
$ ls -l /Volumes
total 44
drwxrwxrwx  29 taylor   staff      986 22 Sep 16:37 110GB
dr-xr-xr-x   4 unknown  nogroup    136 17 Aug  2001 CITIZEN_KANE
drwxrwxrwx  11 taylor   unknown    374  4 Sep 23:28 Extra 30
drwxrwxrwx   1 taylor   admin    16384 19 Aug 20:54 NIKON D100
lrwxr-xr-x   1 root     admin        1 23 Sep 12:30 Panther -> /
drwxrwxr-t  61 root     admin     2074 22 Sep 16:51 X
drwxr-xr-x  15 taylor   unknown    510 27 Apr 09:37 Zephyr
```

Zephyr is the name of the iPod, and NIKON D100 is the camera.

Now, for a neat trick, let's use Unix commands to look at the files on Zephyr:

```
$ ls -F Zephyr
Calendars/              Icon?                   Norton FS Volume
Desktop DB              Norton FS Data          Norton FS Volume 2
Desktop DF              Norton FS Index         iPod_Control/
```

These are the files and directories on the iPod. Where's the music? Let's have a peek in iPod_Control:

```
$ cd Zephyr/iPod_Control/
$ ls -F
Device/         Music/          iPodPrefs*      iTunes/
$ ls -F iTunes
DeviceInfo*             iTunes Temp 3*          iTunesControl*
iTunesPrefs*
iTunes Temp*            iTunes Temp 4*          iTunesDB*
iTunes Temp 1*         iTunes Temp 5*          iTunesEQPresets*
iTunes Temp 2*         iTunes Temp 6*          iTunesPlaylists*
$ ls -F Music
F00/    F02/    F04/    F06/    F08/    F10/    F12/    F14/    F16/    F18/
F01/    F03/    F05/    F07/    F09/    F11/    F13/    F15/    F17/    F19/
$ ls -F Music/F00
A Thousand Years.mp3*               Moody_s Mood For Love.mp3*
African Ripples.mp3*                My One And Only.mp3*
All The Pretty Little Ponie.mp3*    My Thanksgiving.mp3*
Apollo.mp3*                         Nucleus.mp3*
Arrival.mp3*                        Oh_ Yes_ Take Another Guess.mp3*
...
```

So you can see the disk structure the iPod uses and it's completely Unix-friendly: music is stored in the *iPod_Control/Music* directory, and split into directories called *F00* through *F19*.* Within each directory is a set of audio files (mp3, AIFF, AAC, etc.). You can even copy them using the commands we'll discuss in the next chapter. The iPod maintains a difficult-to-manipulate index of the audio files, so you can't add music to your iPod as easily. However, you can make directories in other areas of your iPod and copy files into them, using your iPod as a portable hard drive.

---

* Surprisingly, this disk structure is identical across iPods, regardless of size. It's a compromise between the slow seeks of a single directory for all data and the needless complexity of each album (or artist) having their own subdirectory.

## CHAPTER 4

File Management

Chapter 3 introduced the Unix filesystem, including an extensive discussion of the directory structure and how to move around using cd and pwd. In this chapter, we focus on Unix file naming schemes—which aren't the same as names you'd see in the Finder, as you'll see—and how to rename, edit, copy, and move files. You'll also learn how to use Unix-based file search utilities, which tend to be dramatically faster than Sherlock and other GUI-based find utilities.

File and Directory Names

As Chapter 3 explained, both files and directories are identified by their names. A directory is really just a special kind of file, so the rules for naming directories are the same as the rules for naming files.

Filenames may contain any character except /, which is reserved as the separator between files and directories in a pathname. Filenames are usually made of upper- and lowercase letters, numbers, "." (dots), and "_" (underscores). Other characters (including spaces) are legal in a filename, but they can be hard to use because the shell gives them special meanings. However, spaces are a standard part of Macintosh file and folder names, so while we recommend using only letters, numbers, dots, and underscore characters for filenames, the reality is that you will have to work with spaces in file and directory names. The Finder, by contrast, dislikes colons (which older versions of Mac OS used as a directory separator, just as Unix uses the slash). If you display a file called *test:me* in the Finder, the name is shown as *test/me* instead. (The reverse is also true: if you create a file in the Finder whose name contains a slash, it will appear as a colon in the Terminal.)

Though it's tempting to include spaces in filenames as you do in the Finder, if you're planning on doing any substantial amount of work on the Unix side, get used to using dashes or underscores in lieu of spaces in your filenames. It's 99% as legible, but considerably easier to work with. Further, in the interest of having files correctly identified in both the Finder and Unix, it's a good habit to get into using the appropriate filename suffixes too, i.e., ".doc" for Microsoft Word documents, ".txt" for text files, ".xls" for Excel spreadsheets, and so on. As an added bonus, this makes life easier for your less-fortunate (Windows-using) friends when you send them files.

If you have a file with spaces in its name, the shell will be confused if you type its name on the command line. That's because the shell breaks command lines into separate arguments at the spaces. To tell the shell not to break an argument at spaces, either put quotation marks (") around the argument or preface each space with a backslash (\).

For example, the rm program, covered later in this chapter, removes Unix files. To remove a file named "a confusing name," the first rm command in the following snippet doesn't work, but the second does. Also note that you can escape spaces (that is, avoid having the shell interpret them inappropriately) by using a backslash character, as shown in the third example:

```
$ ls -l
total 2
-rw-r--r--   1 taylor  staff   324 Feb  4 23:07 a confusing name
-rw-r--r--   1 taylor  staff    64 Feb  4 23:07 another odd name
$ rm a confusing name
rm: a: no such file or directory
rm: confusing: no such file or directory
rm: name: no such file or directory
$ rm "a confusing name"
$ rm another\ odd\ name
$
```

You should also use a backslash (\) before any of the following special characters, which have meaning to the shell: * # ` " ' \ $ | & ? ; ~ ( ) < > ! ^.

A filename must be unique inside its directory, but other directories may have files with the same names. For example, you may have the files called *chap1.doc* and *chap2.doc* in the directory */Users/carol/Documents*, and also have different files with the same names in */Users/carol/Desktop*.

File and Directory Wildcards

When you have a number of files named in series (for example, *chap1.doc* to *chap12.doc*) or filenames with common characters (such as *aegis*, *aeon*, and *aerie*), you can use wildcards to specify many files at once. These special characters are * (asterisk), ? (question mark), and [ ] (square brackets). When used in a file or directory name given as an argument on a command line, the characteristics detailed in Table 4-1 are true.

Table 4-1. Shell wildcards

Notation	Definition
*	An asterisk stands for any number of characters in a filename. For example, ae* would match *aegis*, *aerie*, *aeon*, etc. if those files were in the same directory. You can use this to save typing for a single filename (for example, al* for *alphabet.txt*) or to choose many files at once (as in ae*). A * by itself matches all file and subdirectory names in a directory, with the exception of any starting with a period. To match all your dot files, try .??*.
?	A question mark stands for any single character (so h?p matches *hop* and *hip*, but not *help*).
[]	Square brackets can surround a choice of single characters (i.e., one digit or one letter) you'd like to match. For example, [Cc]hapter would match either *Chapter* or *chapter*, but chap[12] would match *chap1* or *chap2*. Use a hyphen (-) to separate a range of consecutive characters. For example, chap[1-3] would match *chap1*, *chap2*, or *chap3*.

The following examples show the use of wildcards. The first command lists all the entries in a directory, and the rest use wildcards to list just some of the entries. The last one is a little tricky; it matches files whose names contain two (or more) *a*'s.

```
$ ls
chap0.txt       chap2.txt       chap5.txt       cold.txt
chap1a.old.txt  chap3.old.txt   chap6.txt       haha.txt
chap1b.txt      chap4.txt       chap7.txt       oldjunk
$ ls chap?.txt
chap0.txt       chap4.txt       chap6.txt
chap2.txt       chap5.txt       chap7.txt
$ ls chap[3-7]*
chat3.old.txt   chap4.txt       chap5.txt       chap6.txt       chap7.txt
$ ls chap??.txt
chap1b.txt
$ ls *old*
chap1a.old.txt  chap3.old.txt   cold.txt        oldjunk
$ ls *a*a*
chap1a.old.txt  haha.txt
```

Wildcards are useful for more than listing files. Most Unix programs accept more than one filename, and you can use wildcards to name multiple files on the command line. For example, both the cat and less programs display files on the screen. cat streams a file's contents until end of file, while less shows the file one screenfull at a time. Let's say you want to display files *chap3.old.txt* and *chap1a.old.txt*. Instead of specifying these files individually, you could enter the command as:

```
$ less *.old.txt
```

This is equivalent to less chap1a.old.txt chap3.old.txt.

Wildcards match directory names, too. You can use them anywhere in a pathname—absolute or relative—though you still need to separate directory levels with slashes (/). For example, let's say you have subdirectories named *Jan, Feb, Mar*, and so on. Each has a file named *summary*. You could read all the summary files by typing less */summary. That's almost equivalent to less Jan/summary Feb/summary. However, there's one important difference when you use less */summary: the names will be alphabetized, so *Apr/summary* would be first in the list.

Creating and Editing Files

One easy way to create a file is with a Unix feature called *input/output redirection*, as Chapter 6 explains. This sends the output of a program directly to a file, to make a new file or add to an existing one.

You'll usually create and edit a plain-text file with a text editor program. Text editors are somewhat different than word processors.

Text Editors and Word Processors

A text editor lets you add, change, and rearrange text easily. Three popular Unix editors included with Mac OS X are *vi* (pronounced "vee-eye"), *Pico*, ("pea-co"), and *Emacs* ("e-max").

You should choose an editor you're comfortable with. vi is probably the best choice because all Unix systems have it, but Emacs is also widely available. If you'll be doing simple editing only, Pico is a great choice. Although Pico is much less powerful than Emacs or vi, it's a lot easier to learn. For this book, however, we'll focus on the rudiments of vi since it's the most widely available Unix editor, and there's a terrific version included with Mac OS X called *vim*.

None of these plain text editors has the same features as popular word-processing software, but vi and Emacs are sophisticated, extremely flexible editors for all kinds of plain-text files: programs, email messages, and so on.

Of course, you can opt to use a graphical text editor such as BBEdit or TextEdit with good results too, if you'd rather just sidestep editing while within the Terminal application. If you do, try using the open command within the Terminal to launch the editor with the proper file already loaded. For example: open -e myfile.txt will open the specified file in TextEdit. One gotcha: you won't see any dot files in the Finder.

Fixing Those Pesky Carriage Returns

The only caveat regarding switching between Finder applications and Unix tools for editing is that you might end up having to translate file formats along the way. Fortunately, this is easy with Unix.

One of the more awkward things about Apple putting a Mac graphical environment on top of a Unix core is that the two systems use different end-of-line character sequences. If you ever open up a file in a Finder application and see lots of little boxes at the end of each line, or if you try to edit a file within Unix and find that it's littered with ^M sequences, you've hit the end-of-line problem.

To fix it, use vi to edit .profile, the tcsh configuration file:

```
$ vi ~/.profile
```

Add the following lines anywhere in the file:

```
alias m2u= "tr '\015' '\012' "
alias u2m="tr '\012' '\015' "
```

Save the file, close your current Terminal window, and open a new one. (Each time you launch a new Terminal window, bash will process the contents of this file.)

Now, whenever you're working with Unix editing tools and you need to fix a Mac-format file, simply use m2u (Mac to Unix), as in:

```
$ m2u < mac-format-file > unix-friendly-file
```

And if you find yourself in the opposite situation, where you're editing a Unix file in a Mac tool and it has some carriage-return weirdness, use the reverse (Unix to Mac) within Terminal before editing:

```
$ u2m < unix-friendly-file > mac-format-file
```

Worthy of note is the helpful tr command, which makes it easy to translate all occurrences of one character to another. Use man tr to learn more about this powerful utility.

By "plain text," we mean a file with only letters, numbers, and punctuation characters in it (text without formatting such as point size, bold and italics, or embedded images). Unix systems use plain-text files in many places: in redirected input and output of Unix programs (see Chapter 6), as shell setup files (see Chapter 1), for shell scripts (see Chapter 10), for system configuration, and more. Text editors edit these files. When you use a word processor, though, although the screen may look as if the file is only plain text, the file probably also has hidden codes (nontext characters) in it. That's often true even if you tell the word processor to "Save as plain text." One easy way to check for nontext characters in a file is by reading the file with less; look for characters in reversed colors, codes such as <36>, and so on.

If you need to do word processing—making documents, envelopes, and so on—your best bet is to work with a program designed for that purpose such as Microsoft Office X, or Panther's all-powerful TextEdit, which can read and write Word files.

The vi Text Editor

The vi editor, originally written by Bill Joy at the University of California, Berkeley, is easy to use once you master the fundamental concept of a modal editor. Mac OS X actually includes a version of vi that has many useful new features, called *vim*. In this section, we cover only its basic commands, but if you become a vi master, you'll enjoy vim's powerful extensions.

Modes can be best explained by thinking about your car stereo. When you have a tape in (or a CD), the "1" button does one task, but if you are listening to the radio, the very same button does something else (perhaps jump to preprogrammed station #1). The vi editor is exactly the same: in *Command mode*, i jumps you into Insert mode, but in *Insert mode* it actually inserts an "i" into the text itself. The handiest key on your keyboard while you're learning vi is unquestionably ESC: if you're in Insert mode, ESC will move you back into Command mode, and if you're in Command mode, it'll beep to let you know that all is well. Use ESC often, until you're completely comfortable keeping track of what mode you're in.

Start vi by typing its name; the argument is the filename you want to create or edit. For instance, to edit your *.profile* setup file, you would cd to your home directory and enter:

```
$ vi .profile
```

The terminal fills with a copy of the file (and, because the file is short, some blank lines too, as denoted by the ~ at the beginning of the line), as shown in Figure 4-1.

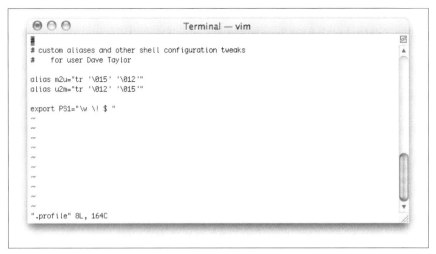

```
  ●  ○  ○                    Terminal — vim
▊
# custom aliases and other shell configuration tweaks
#    for user Dave Taylor

alias m2u="tr '\015' '\012'"
alias u2m="tr '\012' '\015'"

export PS1="\w \! $ "
~
~
~
~
~
~
~
~
".profile" 8L, 164C
```

Figure 4-1. vi display while editing

The bottom row of the window is the status line, which indicates what file you're editing: *".profile" 8L, 164C*. This indicates that the file has eight lines with a total of 164 characters. Quit the program by typing :q and pressing Return while in Command mode.

vi tour

Let's take a tour through vi. In this example, you'll make a new file. You can call the file anything you want, but it's best to use only letters and numbers in the filename. For instance, to make a file named *sample*, enter the command vi sample. Let's start our tour now.

1. Your screen should look something like Figure 4-1, but the cursor should be on the top line and the rest of the lines should have the ~ blank line delimiter. Press i to move out of Command mode and into Insert mode, and you're ready to enter text.

2. Enter some lines of text. Make some lines too short (press Return before the line gets to the right margin). Make others too long; watch how vi wraps long lines. If you have another terminal window open with some text in it, or if you have an Aqua application open, you can also use your mouse to copy text from another window and paste it into the vi window. (Always make sure you're in Insert mode before you do this, however, or you could irrevocably mess up your file.) To get a lot of text quickly, paste the same text more than once.

3. Let's practice moving around the file. To do this, we'll need to leave Insert mode by pressing ESC once. Press it again and you'll hear a beep,

reminding you that you are already in Command mode. You can use your arrow keys to move around the file, but vi also lets you keep your fingers on the keyboard by using h, j, k, and l as the four motion keys (left, down, up, and right, respectively). Unless you have enabled "Option click to position cursor" in Terminal's Preferences, vi will ignore your mouse if you try to use it to move the cursor. If you've entered a lot of text, you can experiment with various movement commands: H to jump to the first line on the screen, G to jump to the bottom of the file. You should also try the w and b commands, to move forward and backward by words. Also, 0 (zero) jumps to the beginning of the line, while $ jumps to the end.

vi's search or "where is" command, /*pattern*, can help you find a word quickly. It's handy even on a short file, where it can be quicker to type / and a word than to use the cursor-moving commands. The search command is also a good example of the way that vi can move your cursor to the status line so you can enter more information. Let's try it by typing /. You should see a display like Figure 4-2.

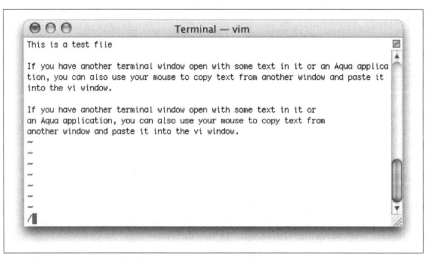

Figure 4-2. vi display while searching

4. Notice that the cursor has jumped to the bottom of the display (which has changed since you started vi) and is sitting next to a /. You can type a word or characters to search for, then press Return to do the search. After a search finishes, you can type n to repeat the search.

5. If your text isn't in paragraphs separated by blank lines, break some of it into paragraphs. Put your cursor at the place you want to break the text, and press i to move back into Insert mode, then press Return twice (once to break the line, another to make a blank line).

6. Now justify one paragraph. Put the cursor at the beginning of the paragraph and type **!}fmt**. (vi's status line won't change until you press the } character.) Now the paragraph's lines should flow and fit neatly between the margins.

7. Text can be deleted by using x to delete the character that's under the cursor, or the powerful d command: dd deletes lines, dw deletes individual words, d$ deletes to the end of the line, d0 deletes to the beginning of the line, and dG deletes to the end of the file (if you're seeing a pattern and thinking that it's d + *motion specifier*, you're absolutely correct). To undo the deletion, press u. You can also paste the deleted text with the p command.

8. The first step to copying text is to position your cursor. The copy command, or "yank," works similar to the delete command. The yw command copies one word, yy yanks the line, y1 a single character, and y*n*w yanks *n* number words. Move the cursor to the line you want to copy and press yy. After repositioning your cursor to where you'd like the text copied, press p to paste the text.

9. As with any text editor, it's a good idea to save your work from vi every 5 or 10 minutes. That way, if something goes wrong on the computer or network, you'll be able to recover the edited buffer since the last time you saved it. When launching vi again, use the -r option with a *filename* to recover the edited buffer where the *filename* is the name of the file you were editing.

   Try writing out your work with :w followed by Return. The bottom of the display will show the filename saved and the number of lines and characters in the file.

   This part confuses some vi beginners. If you want to save the file with the same name it had when you started, just press :w and Return. That's all! You can also choose a different filename: type :w followed by the new filename. Press Return and it's saved.

10. Make one or two more small edits. Then, exit with :q. vi warns you that the file has not been saved. If you want to override the warning, type **:q!**. You can also use a shortcut: :wq writes out your changes and quits vi.

That's it. There's a lot more you can learn about. In Table 4-2, you'll find a handy listing of some of the most common vi commands and their descriptions. O'Reilly has two very helpful books if you want to become a power user: *Learning the vi Editor*, by Linda Lamb and Arnold Robbins, and *vi Editor Pocket Reference*, by Arnold Robbins. Though focused on vi, they offer extensive information about vim as well, and will get you up to speed in no time.

Table 4-2. Common vi editing commands

Command	Meaning
/pattern	Search forward for specified pattern. Repeat search with n.
:q	Quit the edit session.
:q!	Quit, discarding any changes.
:w	Write (save) any changes out to the file.
:wq or ZZ	Write out any changes, then quit (shortcut).
a	Move into Append mode (like Insert mode, but you enter information after the cursor, not before).
b	Move backward one word.
w	Move forward one word.
d1G	Delete from the current point back to the beginning of the file.
dd	Delete the current line.
dG	Delete through end of file.
dw	Delete the following word.
ESC	Move into Command mode.
h	Move backward one character.
l	Move forward one character.
i	Move into Insert mode (ESC moves you back to Command mode).
j	Move down one line.
k	Move up one line.
O	Open up a line above the current line and move into Insert mode.
o	Open up a line below the current line and move into Insert mode.
P	Put (paste) deleted text before the cursor.
p	Put (paste) deleted text after the cursor.
X	Delete character to the left of the cursor.
x	Delete the character under the cursor.
yw	Yank (copy) from the cursor to the end of the current word. You can then paste it with p or P.
yy	Yank (copy) the current line. You can then paste it with p or P.

A Simpler vi Alternative: Pico

If the section on vi has left you longing for the safety and logic of the graphical world, you might want to explore the simple editing alternative of Pico. Originally written as part of a text-based email system called Pine, Pico has taken on a life of its own and is included in many Unix distributions, including Mac OS X. Figure 4-3 shows the test file from the earlier example in Pico.

Pico offers a menu-based approach to editing, with on-screen help. It's a lot friendlier than vi, whose primary way to tell you that you've done something

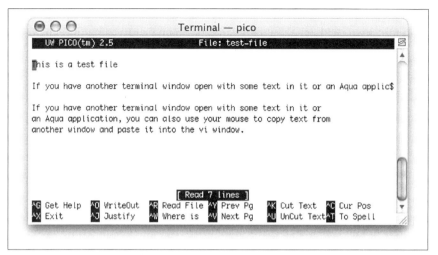

Figure 4-3. Pico, a simpler alternative to vi

wrong is to beep. Pico offers a comfortable middle-ground between text editors such as TextEdit and hardcore Unix text editors such as vi. It's a friendly editor that you can launch from the command line and never have to take your hands off the keyboard to use. To learn more about Pico, type Control-G while within the editor, or use man pico to read the manpage.

Managing Files

The tree structure of the Unix filesystem makes it easy to organize your files. After you make and edit some files, you may want to copy or move files from one directory to another, or rename files to distinguish different versions of a file. You may want to create new directories each time you start a different project. If you copy a file, it's worth learning about the subtle sophistication of the cp and CpMac commands: if you copy a file to a directory, it automatically reuses the filename in the new location. This can save lots of typing!

A directory tree can get cluttered with old files you don't need. If you don't need a file or a directory, delete it to free storage space on the disk. The following sections explain how to make and remove directories and files.

Creating Directories with mkdir

It's handy to group related files in the same directory. If you were writing a spy novel, you probably wouldn't want your intriguing files mixed with restaurant listings. You could create two directories: one for all the chapters in your novel (*spy*, for example), and another for restaurants (*boston.dine*).

To create a new directory, use the mkdir program. The syntax is:

```
mkdir dirname(s)
```

dirname is the name of the new directory. To make several directories, put a space between each directory name. To continue our example, you would enter:

```
$ mkdir spy boston.dine
```

Copying Files

If you're about to edit a file, you may want to save a copy first. That makes it easy to get back the original version. You should use the cp program when copying plain files and directories containing only plain files. Other files having resource forks, such as *Applications*, should be copied with CpMac (available only if you have installed Apple's XCode Tools).

cp

The cp program can put a copy of a file into the same directory or into another directory. cp doesn't affect the original file, so it's a good way to keep an identical backup of a file.

To copy a file, use the command:

```
cp old new
```

where *old* is a pathname to the original file and *new* is the pathname you want for the copy. For example, to copy the */etc/passwd* file into a file called *password* in your working directory, you would enter:

```
$ cp /etc/passwd password
$
```

You can also use the form:

```
cp old olddir
```

This puts a copy of the original file *old* into an existing directory *olddir*. The copy will have the same filename as the original.

If there's already a file with the same name as the copy, cp replaces the old file with your new copy. This is handy when you want to replace an old copy with a newer version, but it can cause trouble if you accidentally overwrite a copy you wanted to keep. To be safe, use ls to list the directory before you make a copy there.

Also, cp has an -i (interactive) option that asks you before overwriting an existing file. It works like this:

```
$ cp -i master existing-file.txt
overwrite existing-file.txt? no
$
```

You can copy more than one file at a time to a single directory by listing the pathname of each file you want copied, with the destination directory at the end of the command line. You can use relative or absolute pathnames (see the section "The Mac OS X Filesystem" in Chapter 3) as well as simple filenames. For example, let's say your working directory is */Users/carol* (from the filesystem diagram in Figure 3-1). To copy three files called *ch1*, *ch2*, and *ch3* from */Users/john* to a subdirectory called *Documents* (that's */Users/carol/Documents*), enter:

```
$ cp ../john/ch1.doc ../john/ch2.doc ../john/ch3.doc Documents
```

Or you could use wildcards and let the shell find all the appropriate files. This time, let's add the -i option for safety:

```
$ cp -i ../john/ch[1-3].doc Documents
cp: overwrite work/ch2.doc ? n
```

There is already a file named *ch2* in the *Documents* directory. When cp asks, answer n to prevent copying *ch2*. Answering y would overwrite the old *ch2*. As you saw in the section "Relative pathnames up" in Chapter 3, the shorthand form . refers to the copy in the working directory, and .. puts it in the parent directory. For example, the following puts the copies into the working directory:

```
$ cp ../john/ch[1-3].doc .
```

One more possibility: when you're working with home directories, you can use a convenient shorthand ~*account* to represent John and Carol's home directory (and ~ by itself to represent your own). So here's yet another way to copy those three files:

```
$ cp ~john/ch[1-3.doc] Documents
```

cp can also copy entire directory trees. Use the option -R, for "recursive." There are two arguments after the option: the pathname of the top-level directory from which you want to copy and the pathname of the place where you want the top level of the copy to be. As an example, let's say that a new employee, Asha, has joined John and Carol. She needs a copy of John's *Documents/work* directory in her own home directory. See the filesystem diagram in Figure 3-1. Her home directory is */Users/asha*. If Asha's own *work* directory doesn't exist yet (important!), she could type the following commands:

```
$ cd /Users
$ cp -R john/Documents/work asha/work
```

Or, from her home directory, she could have typed cp -R ../john/Documents/work work. Either way, she'd now have a new subdirectory */Users/asha/work* with a copy of all files and subdirectories from */Users/john/Documents/work*.

If you give cp -R the wrong pathnames, it can copy a directory tree into itself—running forever until your filesystem
fills up!

Problem checklist

The system says something like "cp: cannot copy file to itself".
> If the copy is in the same directory as the original, the filenames must be
> different.

The system says something like "cp: filename: no such file or directory".
> The system can't find the file you want to copy. Check for a typing mis-
> take. If a file isn't in the working directory, be sure to use its pathname.

The system says something like "cp: permission denied".
> You may not have permission to copy a file created by someone else or
> to copy it into a directory that does not belong to you. Use ls -l to find
> the owner and the permissions for the file, or use ls -ld to check the
> directory. If you feel that you should be able to copy a file, ask the file's
> owner or use *sudo* (see "Superuser Privileges with sudo" in Chapter 3)
> to change its access modes.

Xcode

If you're working with applications and other complex file structures in Mac
OS X, you'll want to have access to CpMac and MvMac, both of which are only
available through Xcode. Fortunately, Xcode is easy to get and install: if you
bought the boxed version of Mac OS X, Xcode should be included on a separate CD-ROM. If you bought a new Macintosh that came with Mac OS X
preinstalled, the Xcode installer will probably be in */Applications/Installers*.
The latest version of the tools are also available to Apple Developer Connection (ADC) members (*http://connect.apple.com/*). Sign up for a free account
and you'll be able to download Xcode and install it yourself!

Copying Mac files with resources

The cp program works on plain files and directories, but the Macintosh system stores applications with resource information. These attributes are
known as *resource forks*, and are used extensively in Classic Mac OS applications and documents. (You will also find them in various places on the
Mac OS X filesystem). If you're a Mac OS 9 veteran, you'll remember that
the resources in the resource fork were only editable with ResEdit, and otherwise were hidden in the system. A file's resource fork, if it exists, can be
seen by looking at a special file called *filename/rsrc*. For example, Microsoft
Word has a resource fork:

```
$ cd /Applications
$ ls -l Microsoft\ Word
-rwxrwxr-x  1 taylor  taylor  10508000  2 Jul 00:00 Microsoft Word
$ ls -l Microsoft\ Word/rsrc
-rwxrwxr-x  1 taylor  taylor  2781444  2 Jul 00:00 Microsoft Word/rsrc
$ cd Microsoft\ Word
```

The preceding listing should appear rather puzzling, actually. The file
Microsoft Word isn't a directory, yet there's a file within as if it were a directory (*rsrc*). But you can't cd into *Microsoft Word* to see the directory. Weird.
Further, if you copy *Microsoft Word* with cp, it won't copy the contents of
the resource fork (in this example, */tmp* is a directory used to hold temporary files):

```
$ cp Microsoft\ Word /tmp
$ ls -l /tmp/Microsoft\ Word
-rwxr-xr-x  1 bjepson  wheel  10568066 Nov 10 14:35 /tmp/Microsoft Word
$ ls -l /tmp/Microsoft\ Word/rsrc
-rwxr-xr-x  1 bjepson  wheel         0 Nov 10 14:35 /tmp/Microsoft Word/rsrc
```

A special version of cp is used to copy files with resource forks. The program, CpMac, is included with XCode.

> If you find yourself using CpMac or MvMac a lot, add */Developer/Tools* to your PATH so you can simply type CpMac rather
> than the full path to the program. PATH is one of a set of environment variables that help the shell keep track of your particular session. Information on customizing your path is
> found in the section "Customizing Your Shell Environment"
> in Chapter 1.

CpMac is found in */Developer/Tools*. To copy *Microsoft Word* and its
resources, invoke the following:

```
$ /Developer/Tools/CpMac Microsoft\ Word /tmp
$ ls -l /tmp/Microsoft\ Word
-rwxrwxrwx  1 bjepson  wheel  10568066 Nov 10 14:37 /tmp/Microsoft Word
$ ls -l /tmp/Microsoft\ Word/rsrc
-rwxrwxrwx  1 bjepson  wheel  2781434 Nov 10 14:37 /tmp/Microsoft Word/rsrc
```

> In addition to resource forks, some files may include HFS
> metadata. A legacy of the earlier Mac OS, HFS metadata
> holds useful information about a file within the first several
> bytes of the file itself. The Mac OS X Finder will still make use
> of some of this data, including creator and type codes that, if
> a document doesn't have a dot extension such as *.mp3*, dictate the file's icon as well as which application should launch
> when you double-click it. A document file that loses this
> metadata might display only a generic icon, and the Finder
> wouldn't know which application to launch it with.

Renaming and Moving Files with mv

To rename a file, use mv (move). The mv program can also move a file from one directory to another.

The mv command has the same syntax as the cp command:

```
mv old new
```

old is the old name of the file and *new* is the new name. mv will write over existing files, which is handy for updating old versions of a file. If you don't want to overwrite an old file, be sure that the new name is unique. The Mac OS X version of mv has an -i option for safety:

```
$ mv chap1.doc intro.doc
$ mv -i chap2.doc intro.doc
mv: overwrite `intro.doc'? n
$
```

The previous example changed the file named *chap1.doc* to *intro.doc*, and then tried to do the same with *chap2.doc* (answering n cancelled the last operation). If you list your files with ls, you will see that the filename *chap1.doc* has disappeared, but *chap2.doc* and *intro.doc* are preserved.

The mv command can also move a file from one directory to another. As with the cp command, if you want to keep the same filename, you need only to give mv the name of the destination directory.

There's also a MvMac command, analogous to the CpMac command explained earlier. Again, check by looking for a */rsrc* resource file before moving and use MvMac if needed.

Finding Files

If your account has lots of files, organizing them into subdirectories can help you find the files later. Sometimes you may not remember which subdirectory has a file. The find program can search for files in many ways; we'll look at two.

Change to your home directory so find will start its search there. Then carefully enter one of the following two find commands. (The syntax is strange and ugly—but find does the job!)

```
$ cd
$ find . -type f -name "chap*" -print
./chap2
./old/chap10b
$ find . -type f -mtime -2 -print
./work/to_do
```

The first command looks in your working directory (.) and all its subdirectories for files (-type f) whose names start with *chap*. (find understands wildcards in filenames. Be sure to put quotes around any filename pattern with a wildcard in it, as we did in the example.) The second command looks for all files that have been created or modified in the last two days (-mtime -2). The relative pathnames that find finds start with a dot (./), the name of the working directory, which you can ignore. Worth noting is that -print displays the results on the screen, not on your printer.

Mac OS X also has the locate program to find files quickly. You can use locate to search part or all of a filesystem for a file with a certain name.

First, you need to build the database of filenames. Use the command:

```
$ sudo /usr/libexec/locate.updatedb
```

It takes a while for this to complete, as it searches through all your directories looking for files and recording their names. This database is automatically rebuilt weekly, but if you ever add a lot of files and want to add them to the database, rerun this command to rebuild the database with the new files.

Once you have the database, search it with the locate command. For instance, if you're looking for a file named *alpha-test*, *alphatest*, or something like that, try this:

```
$ locate alpha
/Users/alan/Desktop/alpha3
/usr/local/projects/mega/alphatest
```

You'll get the absolute pathnames of files and directories with *alpha* in their names. (If you get a lot of output, add a pipe to less. See the section "Piping to a Pager" in Chapter 6.) locate may or may not list protected, private files; its listings usually also aren't completely up to date. The fundamental difference between the two is that find lets you search by file type, contents, and much more, while locate is a simple list of all filenames on the system. To learn much more about find and locate, read their manpages or read the chapter about them in *Mac OS X in a Nutshell* (O'Reilly).

Removing Files and Directories

You may have finished work on a file or directory and see no need to keep it, or the contents may be obsolete. Periodically removing unwanted files and directories frees storage space.

rm

The rm program removes files. Unlike moving an item to the Trash, no opportunity exists to recover the item before you "Empty the Trash" when using rm.

The syntax is simple:

```
rm filename(s)
```

rm removes the named files, as the following example shows:

```
$ ls
chap10          chap2       chap5    cold
chap1a.old      chap3.old   chap6    haha
chap1b          chap4       chap7    oldjunk
$ rm *.old chap10
$ ls
chap1b    chap4    chap6    cold    oldjunk
chap2     chap5    chap7    haha
$ rm c*
$ ls
haha      oldjunk
$
```

When you use wildcards with rm, be sure you're deleting the right files! If you accidentally remove a file you need, you can't recover it unless you have a copy in another directory or in your backups.

Do not enter rm * carelessly. It deletes all the files in your working directory.

Here's another easy mistake to make: you want to enter a command such as rm c* (remove all filenames starting with "c"), but instead enter rm c * (remove the file named c and all files!).

It's good practice to list the files with ls before you remove them. Or, if you use rm's -i (interactive) option, rm asks you whether you want to remove each file.

rmdir

Just as you can create new directories with mkdir, you can remove them with the rmdir program. As a precaution, rmdir won't let you delete directories that contain any files or subdirectories; the directory must first be empty. (The rm -r command removes a directory and everything in it. It can be dangerous for beginners, though.)

The syntax is:

```
rmdir dirname(s)
```

If a directory you try to remove does contain files, you get a message like "rmdir: *dirname* not empty".

To delete a directory that contains some files:

1. Enter cd *dirname* to get into the directory you want to delete.
2. Enter rm * to remove all files in that directory.
3. Enter cd .. to go to the parent directory.
4. Enter rmdir *dirname* to remove the unwanted directory.

Problem checklist

I still get the message "dirname not empty" even after I've deleted all the files.

Use ls -a to check that there are no hidden files (names that start with a period) other than . and .. (the working directory and its parent). The following command is good for cleaning up hidden files (which aren't matched by a simple wildcard such as *). It matches all hidden files except for . (the current directory) and .. (the parent directory):

```
$ rm -i .[^.]*
```

Working with Links

If you've used the Mac for a while, you're familiar with aliases, empty files that point to other files on the system. A common use of aliases is to have a copy of an application on the desktop, or to have a shortcut in your home directory. Within the graphical environment, you make aliases by using ⌘-Click and then choosing Make Alias from the context menu. The result of an alias, in Unix, looks like this:

```
$ ls -l *3*
-rw-r--r--  1 taylor  taylor  1546099 23 Sep 20:58 fig0403.pdf
-rw-r--r--  1 taylor  taylor        0 24 Sep 08:34 fig0403.pdf alias
```

In this case, the file *fig0403.pdf alias* is an Aqua alias pointing to the actual file *fig0403.pdf* in the same directory. But you wouldn't know it because it appears to be an empty file: the size is shown as zero bytes.

Unix works with aliases differently; on the Unix side, we talk about links, not aliases. There are two types of links possible in Unix, hard links or symbolic links, and both are created with the ln command.

The syntax is:

```
ln [-s] source target
```

The −s flag indicates that you're creating a symbolic link, so to create a second file that links to the file *fig0403.pdf*, the command would be:

```
$ ln -s fig0403.pdf neato-pic.pdf
```

and the results would be:

```
$ ls -l *pdf
-rw-r--r--  1 taylor  taylor  1532749 23 Sep 20:47 fig0401.pdf
-rw-r--r--  1 taylor  taylor  1539493 23 Sep 20:52 fig0402.pdf
-rw-r--r--  1 taylor  taylor  1546099 23 Sep 20:58 fig0403.pdf
lrwxr-xr-x 1 taylor  taylor       18 24 Sep 08:40 neato-pic.pdf@ ->
     fig0403.pdf
```

One way to think about symbolic links is that they're akin to a Stickies note saying "the info you want isn't here, it's in file X." This also implies a peculiar behavior of symbolic links (and Aqua aliases): move, rename, or remove the item being pointed to and you have an orphan link. The system doesn't remove or update symbolic links automatically.

The other type of link is a hard link, which essentially creates a second name entry for the exact same contents. That is, if we create a hard link to *fig0403. pdf*, we can then delete the original file, and the contents remain accessible through the second filename—they're different doors into the same room (as opposed to a Sticky left on a door telling you to go to the second door instead, as would be the case with a symbolic link). Hard links are created by omitting the –s flag:

```
$ ln mypic.pdf copy2.pdf
$ ls -l mypic.pdf copy2.pdf
-rw-r--r--  2 taylor  taylor  1546099 24 Sep 08:45 copy2.pdf
-rw-r--r--  2 taylor  taylor  1546099 24 Sep 08:45 mypic.pdf
$ rm mypic.pdf
$ ls -l copy2.pdf
-rw-r--r--  1 taylor  taylor  1546099 24 Sep 08:45 copy2.pdf
```

Notice that both files are exactly the same size when the hard link is created. This makes sense because they're both names to the same underlying set of data, so they should be completely identical. Then, when the original is deleted, the data survives with the second name now as its only name.

Compressing and Archiving Files

Aqua users may commonly use StuffIt's *.sit* and *.hqx* formats for file archives, but Unix users have many other options worth exploring. There are three compression programs included with Mac OS X, though the most popular is gzip (the others are compress and bzip2; read their manpages to learn more about how they differ). There's also a very common Unix archive format called tar that we'll cover briefly.

gzip

Though it may initially confuse you into thinking that it's part of the Zip archive toolset, gzip is actually a compression program that does a very good job of shrinking down individual files for storage and transmission. If you're sending a file to someone with a dial-up connection, for example, running the file through gzip can significantly reduce its size and make it much more portable. Just as importantly, it can help save space on your disk by letting you compress files you want to keep, but aren't using currently. gzip works particularly well with tar too, as you'll see.

The syntax is:

```
gzip [-v] file(s)
```

The –v flag offers verbose output, letting the program indicate how much space it saved by compressing the file. Very useful information, as you may expect!

```
$ ls -l ch06.doc
-rwxr-xr-x  1 taylor  taylor  138240 24 Sep 08:52 ch06.doc
$ gzip -v ch06.doc
ch06.doc:                   75.2% -- replaced with ch06.doc.gz
$ ls -l ch06.doc.gz
-rwxr-xr-x  1 taylor  taylor  34206 24 Sep 08:52 ch06.doc.gz
```

You can see that gzip did a great job compressing the file, saving over 75%. Notice that it's automatically appended a *.gz* filename suffix to indicate that the file is now compressed. To uncompress the file, just use gunzip:

```
$ gunzip ch06.doc.gz
$ ls -l ch06.doc
-rwxr-xr-x  1 taylor  taylor  138240 24 Sep 08:52 ch06.doc
```

tar

In the old days, Unix system backups were done to streaming tape devices (today you can only see them in cheesy 60s scifi films, the huge round tape units that randomly spin as data is accessed). The tool of choice for creating backups from Unix systems onto these streaming tape devices was tar, the tape archiver. Fast forward to Mac OS X, and tar continues to be a useful utility, but now it's used to create files that contain directories and other files within, as an archive. It's similar to the Zip format, but differs from gzip because its job is to create a file that contains multiple files. gzip, by contrast, makes an existing file shrink as much as possible through compression.

The tar program is particularly helpful when combined with gzip, actually, because it makes creating archive copies of directories simple and effective. Even better, if you use the –z flag to tar, it automatically invokes gzip to compress its output without any further work.

The syntax is:

```
tar [c|t|x] [flags] files and directories to archive
```

The tar program is too complex to fully explain here, but in a nutshell, tar -c creates archives, tar -t shows what's in an existing archive, and tar -x extracts files and directories from an archive. The –f *file* flag is used to specify the archive name, and the –v flag offers verbose output to let you see what's going on. As always, man tar will produce lots more information.

```
$ du -s Masters\ Thesis/
6704    Masters Thesis/
$ tar -czvf masters.thesis.tgz Masters\ Thesis
Masters Thesis/
Masters Thesis/.DS_Store
Masters Thesis/analysis.doc
...
Masters Thesis/Web Survey Results.doc
Masters Thesis/web usage by section.doc
$ ls -l masters.thesis.tgz
-rw-r--r--  1 taylor  staff  853574 24 Sep 09:20 masters.thesis.tgz
```

In this example, the directory *Masters Thesis* is 6.7 MB in size, and hasn't been accessed in quite a while. This makes it a perfect candidate for a compressed tar archive. This is done by combining the –c (create) –z (compress with gzip) –v (verbose) and –f *file* (output file; notice that we added the *.gz* suffix to avoid later confusion about the file type). In under 10 seconds, a new archive file is created, which is less than 1 MB in size, yet contains all the files and directories in the original archive. To unpack the archive, we'd use tar -xvfz masters.thesis.tgz.

 Notice that we gave tar the directory name, rather than a list of files. This ensures that when the directory is unpacked, the files will be put in a new directory (*Masters Thesis*), rather than filling the current directory. This is a good habit for people who make lots of archives.

Files on Other Operating Systems

Chapter 8 includes the section "Transferring Files," which explains ways to transfer files across a network—possibly to non-Unix operating systems. Mac OS X has the capability of connecting to a variety of different filesystems remotely, including Microsoft Windows, other Unix systems, and even web-based filesystems.

If the Windows-format filesystem is mounted with your other filesystems, you'll be able to use its files by typing a Unix-like pathname. If you've mounted a remote Windows system's *C:* drive over a share named *winc*, you can access the Windows file *C:\WORD\REPORT.DOC* through the pathname */Volumes/winc/word/report.doc*. Indeed, most external volumes are automatically mounted within the */Volumes* directory.

## CHAPTER 5

Printing

Working in the Macintosh environment, you're used to a simple and elegant printer interface, particularly in Mac OS X, where the Printer Setup Utility makes it a breeze to add new printers and configure your existing printers. Until the advent of the Common Unix Printing System (CUPS), the Unix environment has never had a printing interface that even comes close in usability. As of Mac OS X 10.3, the Printer Setup Utility and CUPS are combined in a way that brings joy to command-line and GUI lovers alike.

Add a printer with Printer Setup Utility, and you'll have access to hundreds of different printer models that are supported in Panther. The Linux Printing archive has even more Mac OS X compatible drivers (*http://www.linuxprinting.org/*).

Formatting and Print Commands

Before you print a file on a Unix system, you may want to reformat it to adjust the margins, highlight some words, and so on. Most files can also be printed without reformatting, but the raw print out might not look quite as nice. Further, some printers accept only PostScript, which means you'll need to use a text-to-PostScript filter such as enscript for good results. Before we cover printing itself, let's look at both pr and enscript to see how they work.

PostScript is a page-description language from Adobe supported by some printer models. PostScript printers were once the norm among Macintosh users and are still popular. If you're using an inexpensive USB inkjet printer or a low- to mid-range laser printer, chances are good that your printer doesn't support PostScript. Some of the utilities described in this section require PostScript, others don't. Refer to your printer's documentation (or the manufacturer's web site) to ascertain whether your printer supports PostScript.

If you don't have a PostScript printer and are working in Unix, don't despair: almost all of Unix is text-oriented, so even a basic inkjet printer will be able to print code listings, simple email messages, and manpages without a hiccup.

pr

The pr program does minor formatting of files on the Terminal or for a printer. For example, if you have a long list of names in a file, you can format it onscreen into two or more columns.

The syntax is:

```
pr option(s) filename(s)
```

pr changes the format of the file only on the screen or on the printed copy; it doesn't modify the original file. Table 5-1 lists some pr options.

Table 5-1. Some pr options

Option	Description
-k	Produces k columns of output
-d	Double-spaces the output
-h *header*	Prints *header* at top of each page
-t	Eliminates printing of header and top/bottom margins

Other options allow you to specify the width of columns, set the page length, etc. For a complete list of options, see the manpage, man pr.

Before using pr, here are the contents of a sample file named *food*:

```
$ cat food
Sweet Tooth
Bangkok Wok
Mandalay
Afghani Cuisine
Isle of Java
Big Apple Deli
Sushi and Sashimi
Tio Pepe's Peppers
$
```

Let's use pr options to make a two-column report with the header "Restaurants":

```
$ pr -2 -h "Restaurants" food

Sep 24 12:41 2003 Restaurants Page 1
Sweet Tooth                     Isle of Java
Bangkok Wok                     Big Apple Deli
```

```
Mandalay                          Sushi and Sashimi
Afghani Cuisine                   Tio Pepe's Peppers.
.
.
$
```

The text is output in two-column pages. The top of each page has the date and time, header (or name of the file, if a header is not supplied), and page number. To send this output to the default Mac OS X printer instead of to the terminal screen, create a pipe to the lpr printer program:

```
$ pr -2 -h "Restaurants" food | lpr
```

See the section "Pipes and Filters" in Chapter 6 for more information on pipes. The lpr program will be discussed in more detail later in this chapter.

pr does not require a PostScript printer.

enscript

One reason for the success of the Macintosh is its integrated support of Post-Script for printing. Allowing sophisticated imaging and high-quality text, PostScript printers are the norm in the Mac world. However, this proves a bit of a problem from the Unix perspective, because Unix commands are used to working with regular text without any special PostScript formatting included.

Translating plain text into PostScript is the job of enscript. The enscript program has a remarkable number of different command flags, allowing you access to all the layout and configuration options you're familiar with from the Page Setup and Print dialog boxes in Aqua.

The most helpful command flags are summarized in Table 5-2 (you can learn about all the many options to enscript by reading the enscript manpage). A typical usage is to send the file to a printer:

```
$ enscript -p - Sample.txt | lpr
[ 1 pages * 1 copy ] left in -
$
```

Enscript can also produce PostScript output files for distribution in electronic form: enscript -psample.eps sample.txt translates *sample.txt* into PostScript and saves the resultant output to the file *sample.eps*.

Table 5-2. Useful enscript options

Option	Description
-B	Do not print page headers.
-f *font*	Print body text using *font* (the default is Courier10).

Table 5-2. Useful enscript options (continued)

Option	Description
-j	Print borders around columns (you can turn on multicolumn output with -1 or -2).
-p *file*	Send output to *file*. Use - to stream output to standard out (for pipes).
-r	Rotate printout 90 degrees, printing in landscape mode instead of portrait (the default).
-W *lang*	Output in the specified language. Default is PostScript, but enscript also supports HTML, overstrike, and RTF.

lpr

The underlying printing command in Unix is the command lpr, which sends files or the input stream to your default printer (as chosen using the Printer Setup Utility). The syntax is:

> lpr *option(s) filename(s)*

After you enter the command to print a file, the shell prompt returns to the screen and you can enter another command. However, seeing the prompt doesn't mean your file has been printed. Your file has been added to the printer queue to be printed in turn.

To print a file named *bills* on the default printer, use the lpr command, as in this example:

```
$ lpr bills
$
```

lpr has no output if everything was accepted and queued properly. If you need ID numbers for lpr jobs, use the lpq program to view the print queue (see the section "lpq" later in this chapter). The file *bills* will be sent to the default system printer. lpr has a number of options, most of which aren't useful in the Mac OS X Unix environment. Table 5-3 lists the most useful of them.

Table 5-3. The most useful lpr options

Command	Description
-P*printer*	Use given *printer* name if there is more than one printer at your site. The printer names are assigned in Printer Setup Utility.
-#	Print # copies of the file.
-C*name*	Specify job name.
-p	Print file should be formatted with a shaded information header containing filename, date, time, and page number. Useful only with text files.
-r	Files printed should be deleted after completion of printing task (only for named files).

Problem checklist

lpr returns "jobs queued, but cannot start daemon".
> Your system is probably not configured properly for an lpr printer. If you have a named lpr printer that works, try the command again with the -Pprintername option. If not, double check that your printer is set up and chosen as the default printer in Printer Setup Utility. You might want to try using atprint or opening up your files in TextEdit and printing from the Aqua environment.

My printout hasn't come out.
> See whether the printer is printing now. If it is, other users may have made requests to the same printer ahead of you, and your file should be printed in turn. The following section explains how to check the print requests. Use the lpq command to ensure that it's still in the queue too.
>
> If no file is printing, check the printer's paper supply, physical connections, and power switch. The printer may also be hung (stalled). If it is, ask other users or system staff people for advice.

My printout is garbled or doesn't look anything like the file did on my terminal.
> The printer may not be configured to handle the kind of file you're printing. For instance, a file in plain-text format will look fine when previewed in your Terminal window, but look like gibberish when you try to print it. If the printer understands only PostScript, make sure that you use enscript to translate the plain-text format into acceptable PostScript.

lpr does not require a PostScript printer.

Viewing the Printer Queue

If you want to find out how many files or "requests" for output are ahead of yours in the printer queue, use the program lpq. The lprm command lets you cancel print jobs from the lpr queue.

Remember that you can also check on the status of print jobs by going into Applications → Utilities → Printer Setup Utility. Double-click on the printer to see the state of the queue.

lpq

The lpq command shows what's currently printing and what's in the queue for the default printer:

```
$ lpq
LaserJet is ready and printing
```

```
Rank    Owner   Job   File(s)                       Total Size
1st     taylor  5     (stdin)                       1024 bytes
2nd     taylor  6     Microsoft Word - ch05.doc     190464 bytes
3rd     taylor  8     TINTIN.COM                    30720 bytes
$
```

The first line displays the printer status. If the printer is disabled or out of paper, you may see different messages on this first line. Here you can see that the printer is ready for new print jobs and is currently printing. Jobs are printed in the order indicated in the lpq output. The Job number is important, because you can remove print jobs from the queue (if you're the owner) with lprm.

lprm

lprm terminates lpr requests. You can specify either the ID of the request (displayed by lpq) or the name of the printer.

If you don't have the request ID, get it from lpq, then use lprm. Specifying the request ID cancels the request, even if it is currently printing:

```
$ lprm 8
```

To cancel whatever request is currently printing, regardless of its ID, simply enter lprm and the printer name:

```
$ lprm LaserJet
```

lprm does not provide any feedback unless it encounters an error.

Working with AppleTalk Printers

If you have an AppleTalk-based printer, or want to use a network printer that's accessible on your AppleTalk network, there is a set of easy-to-use AppleTalk-aware Unix commands included with Mac OS X. The most important of the commands is atprint, which lets you easily stream any Unix output to a printer.

To start working with the AppleTalk tools, run atlookup, which lists all the AppleTalk devices recognized on the network (and that can be quite a few):

```
$ atlookup
Found 4 entries in zone *
ff41.d0.80      Dave Taylor's Computer:Darwin
ff01.04.08      LJ2100TN-via-AppleTalk:SNMP Agent
ff01.04.9d      LJ2100TN-via-AppleTalk:LaserWriter
ff01.04.9e      LJ2100TN-via-AppleTalk:LaserJet 2100
```

You can see that the LJ2100TN printer (an HP LaserJet2100) appears with two different AppleTalk addresses. Fortunately, that can safely be ignored as well as the other AppleTalk devices that show up in the list. The important thing is that the `atlookup` command confirmed that there is indeed an Apple-Talk printer online.

To select a specific AppleTalk printer as the default printer for the `atprint` command, run the oddly named at_cho_prn command. The trick is that you need to run this command as *root* or administrator. Use the sudo command (see "Superuser Privileges with sudo" in Chapter 3) to run the program as *root*:

```
$ sudo at_cho_prn
Password:
Zone:*??????@??`??Pp??????@??`??RH?????????RP?
  1: ff01.04.9dtLJ2100TN-via-AppleTalk:LaserWriter

ITEM number (0 to make no selection)?1
Default printer is:LJ2100TN-via-AppleTalk:LaserWriter@*
status: idle
```

If you are on a multizone network, you'll be prompted to select a zone first.

Now, finally, the LaserJet 2100 printer is selected as the default AppleTalk printer, and all subsequent invocations of `atprint` will be sent to that printer without having to remember its exact name.

Because most of the printers available through AppleTalk on a Macintosh network are PostScript printers, it's essential to use the enscript program to ensure the output is in proper PostScript format. As an example, the following prints the intro manpage (an introduction to the manpage system) on the LaserWriter printer, properly translated into PostScript:

```
$ man intro | enscript -p - | atprint
Looking for LJ2100TN-via-AppleTalk:LaserWriter@*.
Trying to connect to LJ2100TN-via-AppleTalk:LaserWriter@*.
[ 1 pages * 1 copy ] left in -
atprint: printing on LJ2100TN-via-AppleTalk:LaserWriter@*.
$
```

Pipes (command sequences with a pipe (|) between the commands) are covered in more detail in Chapter 6.

`atprint` does not require a PostScript printer (unless used with enscript), but it does require an AppleTalk printer.

Non-PostScript Printers

Before Mac OS X 10.3 Panther, the lpr command could handle a variety of file types (including PDF, plain text, and many image types), but not Post-Script, unless you had a PostScript printer. If your printer does not support

PostScript, you will not be able to use lpr to print PostScript files directly. This also means that you won't be able to use enscript for printing.

However, if you've installed Fink (see "Fink" in Chapter 9), you can install the ghostscript package and run ps2pdf to turn your PostScript file into a PDF. To run enscript on the *food* file, convert it to PDF and print it, using pipes between enscript, ps2pdf, and lpr:

```
$ enscript -o - food | ps2pdf - - | lpr
```

The -o - switches and the pipe symbol (|) tell enscript to send its Post-Script output to the ps2pdf program. The - - options and the pipe tell ps2pdf to read its input from the pipe and send its output to lpr, which sends the PDF to the printer. For more information on pipes, see Chapter 6.

Redirecting I/O

Many Unix programs read input (such as a file) and write output in a standard way that lets them work with each other. In this chapter, we discuss some of these tools and learn how to connect programs and files in new and powerful ways.

This chapter generally *doesn't* apply to full-screen programs, such as the vi editor, that take control of your whole Terminal window. (less and more do work together in this way, however.) It also doesn't apply to graphical programs, such as the Finder or Safari, that open their own windows on your screen.

Standard Input and Standard Output

What happens if you don't give a filename argument on a command line? Most programs will take their input from your keyboard instead (after you press Return to start the program running, that is). Your Terminal keyboard is the program's *standard input*.

As a program runs, the results are usually displayed on your Terminal screen. The Terminal screen is the program's *standard output*. So, by default, each of these programs takes its information from the standard input and sends the results to the standard output. These two default cases of input/output (I/O) can be varied. This is called *I/O redirection*.

If a program writes to its standard output, which is normally the screen, you can make it write to a file instead by using the greater-than symbol (>) operator. The pipe operator (|) sends the standard output of one program to the standard input of another program. Input/output redirection is one of the most powerful and flexible Unix features.

If a program doesn't normally read from files, but reads from its standard input, you can give a filename by using the less-than symbol (<) operator. tr (character translator) is such a program. Here's how to use the input redirection operator to convert commas to linefeeds in the *to_do* file:

```
$ cat to_do
Install Mac OS X,Learn Unix,???,Profit!
$ tr ',' '\n' < to_do
Install Mac OS X
Learn Unix
???
Profit!
$
```

Can you see what's happened here? The tr command has translated every comma in the input file (*to_do*, which replaced standard input because of the < notation) to a carriage return, displaying the output on standard output (the Terminal window).

Putting Text in a File

Instead of always letting a program's output come to the screen, you can redirect output to a file. This is useful when you'd like to save program output or when you put files together to make a bigger file.

cat

cat, which is short for "concatenate," reads files and outputs their contents one after another, without stopping.

To display files on the standard output (your screen), use:

    cat *file(s)*

For example, let's display the contents of the file */etc/bashrc*. This system file is the global login file for *bassh*:

```
$ cat /etc/bashrc
# System-wide .bashrc file for interactive bash(1) shells.
PS1='\h:\w \u\$ '
$
```

You cannot go back to view the previous screens, as you can when you use a pager program such as less (unless you're using a Terminal window with a sufficient scrollback buffer, that is). cat is mainly used with redirection, as we'll see in a moment.

By the way, if you enter cat without a filename, it tries to read from the keyboard (as we mentioned earlier). You can get out by pressing Control-D.

When you add > *filename* to the end of a command line, the program's output is diverted from the standard output to a file. The > symbol is called the *output redirection operator*.

When you use the > operator, be careful not to accidentally overwrite a file's contents. Your system may let you redirect output to an existing file. If so, the old file's contents will be lost forever (or, in Unix lingo, "clobbered"). Be careful not to overwrite a much needed file!

Many shells can protect you from the risk. In bash (the default shell for Mac OS X), use the command set noclobber. Enter the command at a shell prompt or put it in your ~/.profile file. After that, the shell won't allow you to redirect onto an existing file and overwrite its contents.

This doesn't protect against overwriting by Unix programs such as cp; it works only with the > redirection operator. For more protection, you can set Unix file access permissions (see Chapter 4).

For example, let's use cat with the output redirection operator. The file contents that you'd normally see on the screen (from the standard output) are diverted into another file, which we'll then read using cat (without any redirection!):

```
$ cat /etc/bashrc > mybashrc
$ cat mybashrc
# System-wide .bashrc file for interactive bash(1) shells.
PS1='\h:\w \u\$ '
$
```

An earlier example showed how cat /etc/bashrc displays the file */etc/bashrc* on the screen. The example here adds the > operator, so the output of cat goes to a file called *mybashrc* in the working directory. Displaying the file *mybashrc* shows that its contents are the same as the file */etc/bashrc* (the effect is the same as the copy command cp /etc/bashrc mybashrc).

You can use the > redirection operator with any program that sends text to its standard output—not just with cat. For example:

```
$ who > users
$ date > today
$ ls
mylogin   today   users   ...
```

We've sent the output of who to a file called *users* and the output of date to the file named *today*. Listing the directory shows the two new files. Let's look at the output from the who and date programs by reading these two files with cat:

```
$ cat users
taylor    console   Sep 24 07:58
taylor    ttyp1     Sep 24 08:00
$ cat today
Wed Sep 24 09:41:07 MDT 2003
$
```

You can also use the cat program and the > operator to make a small text file. We told you earlier to type Control-D if you accidentally enter cat without a filename. This is because the cat program alone takes whatever you type on the keyboard as input. Thus, the command:

```
cat > filename
```

takes input from the keyboard and redirects it to a file. Try the following example:

```
$ cat > to_do
Finish report by noon
Lunch with Xian
Swim at 5:30
^D
$
```

cat takes the text that you typed as input (in this example, the three lines that begin with Finish, Lunch, and Swim), and the > operator redirects it to a file called *to_do*. Type Control-D *once*, on a new line by itself, to signal the end of the text. You should get a shell prompt.

You can also create a bigger file from smaller files with the cat command and the > operator. The form:

```
cat file1 file2 > newfile
```

creates a file *newfile*, consisting of *file1* followed by *file2*.

```
$ cat today to_do > diary
$ cat diary
Wed Sep 24 09:41:07 MDT 2003
Finish report by noon
Lunch with Xian
Swim at 5:30
$
```

You shouldn't use redirection to add a file to itself, along with other files. For example, you might hope that the following command would merge today's to-do list with tomorrow's. This isn't a good idea.

```
$ cat to_do to_do.tomorrow > to_do.tomorrow
```

It works, but it runs for all eternity because it keeps copying the file over itself. If you cancel it with Control-C, and use ls to examine the file, you'll see that it's gotten quite large:

```
^C
```

```
$ ls -sk to_do.tomorrow
```

```
81704 to_do.tomorrow
```

ls -sk shows the size in kilobytes, so it grew to about 80 megabytes! The right way to do this is either to use a temporary file (as you'll see in a later example) or simply to use a text editor program.

You can add more text to the end of an existing file, instead of replacing its contents, by using the >> (append redirection) operator. Use it as you would the > (output redirection) operator. So, the following:

```
cat file2 >> file1
```

appends the contents of *file2* to the end of *file1*. This doesn't affect the contents of *file2*: it is being read from, not written to.

For an example, let's append the contents of the file *users* and the current date and time to the file *diary*. Here's what it looks like:

```
$ cat users >> diary
$ date >> diary
$ cat diary
Wed Sep 24 09:41:07 MDT 2003
Finish report by noon
Lunch with Xian
Swim at 5:30
taylor    console  Nov 11 22:06
taylor    ttyp1    Nov 15 08:16
Wed Sep 24 11:21:35 MDT 2003
$
```

Unix doesn't have a redirection operator that adds text to the beginning of a file. You can do this by storing the new text in a temporary file, then using a text editor program to read the temporary file into the start of the file you want to edit. You also can do the job with a temporary file and redirection. Maybe you'd like each day's entry to go at the beginning of your *diary* file. Simply rename *diary* to something like *temp*. Make a new *diary* file with today's entries, then append *temp* (with its old contents) to the new *diary*. For example:

```
$ mv diary temp
$ date > diary
$ cat users >> diary
$ cat temp >> diary
$ rm temp
```

This example could be shortened by combining the two cat commands into one, giving both filenames as arguments to a single cat command. That wouldn't work, though, if you were making a real diary with a command other than cat users.

Pipes and Filters

We've seen how to redirect input from a file and output to a file. You can also connect two *programs* together so that the output from one program becomes the input of the next program. Two or more programs connected in this way form a *pipe*. To make a pipe, put a vertical bar (|) on the command line between two commands. When a pipe is set up between two commands, the standard output of the command to the left of the pipe symbol becomes the standard input of the command to the right of the pipe symbol. Any two commands can form a pipe as long as the first program writes to standard output and the second program reads from standard input.

When a program takes its input from another program, performs some operation on that input, and writes the result to the standard output (which may be piped to yet another program), it is referred to as a *filter*. A common use of filters is to modify output. Just as a common filter culls unwanted items, Unix filters can restructure output.

Most Unix programs can be used to form pipes. Some programs that are commonly used as filters are described in the next sections. Note that these programs aren't used only as filters or parts of pipes. They're also useful on their own.

grep

The grep program searches the contents of files for lines that have a certain pattern. The syntax is:

```
grep "pattern" file(s)
```

The name "grep" is derived from the ed (a Unix line editor) command g/ re/p, which means "globally search for a regular expression and print all matching lines containing it." A *regular expression* is either some plain text (a word, for example) or special characters used for pattern matching. When you learn more about regular expressions, you can use them to specify complex patterns of text.

 grep understands plain text and that's all. The Find command in the Finder can meaningfully search Microsoft Word data files, for example, but grep knows text only. Feeding it non-text files can produce puzzling and peculiar results. For example, Word files and a lot of other application data contain characters that, when sent to *Terminal.app*, mess up your display in strange and interesting ways. One way to search such files from the command line is to extract only the printable characters using the strings program (see man strings for details).

The simplest use of grep is to look for a pattern consisting of a single word. It can be used in a pipe so only those lines of the input files containing a given string are sent to the standard output. But let's start with an example reading from files: searching all files in the working directory for a word—say, *Unix*. We'll use the wildcard * to quickly give grep all filenames in the directory.

```
$ grep "Unix" *
ch01:Unix is a flexible and powerful operating system
ch01:When the Unix designers started work, little did
ch05:What can we do with Unix?
$
```

When grep searches multiple files, it shows the filename where it finds each matching line of text. Alternatively, if you don't give grep a filename to read, it reads its standard input; that's the way all filter programs work:

```
$ ls -l | grep "Jan"
drwx------    4 taylor  taylor   264  Jan 29 22:33 Movies/
drwx------    2 taylor  taylor   264  Jan 13 10:02 Music/
drwx------   95 taylor  taylor  3186  Jan 29 22:44 Pictures/
drwxr-xr-x    3 taylor  taylor   264  Jan 24 21:24 Public/
$
```

First, the example runs ls -l to list your directory. The standard output of ls -l is piped to grep, which outputs only lines that contain the string Jan (that is, files or directories that were last modified in January and any other lines that have the pattern "Jan" within). Because the standard output of grep isn't redirected, those lines go to the Terminal screen.

grep options let you modify the search. Table 6-1 lists some of the options.

Table 6-1. Some grep options

Option	Description
-v	Print all lines that do not match pattern.
-n	Print the matched line and its line number.
-l	Print only the names of files with matching lines (lowercase letter "L").
-c	Print only the count of matching lines.
-i	Match either upper- or lowercase.

Next, let's use a regular expression that tells grep to find lines with *root*, followed by zero or more other characters (abbreviated in a regular expression as .*), then followed by Jan:

```
$ ls -l | grep "root.*Jan"
drwxr-xr-x  12 root    staff    364 Jan  9 20:24 NetInfo/
$
```

Note that the regular expression for "zero or more characters," .*, is different than the corresponding filename wildcard *. See the section "File and Directory Wildcards" in Chapter 4. We can't cover regular expressions in enough depth here to explain the difference, though more-detailed books do. As a rule of thumb, remember that the first argument to grep is a regular expression; other arguments, if any, are filenames that can use wildcards.

For more about regular expressions, see the references in the section "Documentation" in Chapter 10.

sort

The sort program arranges lines of text alphabetically or numerically. The following example sorts the lines in the *food* file (from the section "pr" in Chapter 5) alphabetically. sort doesn't modify the file itself; it just reads the file and displays the result on standard output (in this case, the Terminal).

```
$ sort food
Afghani Cuisine
Bangkok Wok
Big Apple Deli
Isle of Java
Mandalay
Sushi and Sashimi
Sweet Tooth
Tio Pepe's Peppers
```

By default, sort arranges lines of text alphabetically. Many options control the sorting, and Table 6-2 lists some of them.

Table 6-2. Some sort options

Option	Description
-n	Sort numerically (for example, 10 sorts after 2); ignore blanks and tabs.
-r	Reverse the sorting order.
-f	Sort upper- and lowercase together.
+x	Ignore first x fields when sorting.

More than two commands may be linked up into a pipe. Taking a previous pipe example using grep, we can further sort the files modified in January by order of size. The following pipe uses the commands ls, grep, and sort:

```
$ ls -l | grep "Jan" | sort +4n
drwx------    2 taylor taylor  264  Jan 13 10:02 Music/
drwx------    4 taylor taylor  264  Jan 29 22:33 Movies/
drwxr-xr-x   3 taylor taylor  264  Jan 24 21:24 Public/
drwx------   95 taylor taylor 3186  Jan 29 22:44 Pictures/
$
```

This pipe sorts all files in your directory modified in January by order of size, and prints them to the Terminal screen. The sort option +4n skips 4 fields (fields are separated by blanks), then sorts the lines in numeric order. So, the output of ls, filtered by grep, is sorted by the file size (this is the fifth column, starting with 264). Both grep and sort are used here as filters to modify the output of the ls -l command. You could print the listing by piping the sort output to your printer command (either lp, lpr, or atprint).

Piping to a Pager

The less program, which you saw in the section "Looking Inside Files with less" in Chapter 3, can also be used as a filter. A long output normally zips by you on the screen, but if you run text through less, the display stops after each page or screenfull of text (that's why they're called "pagers": they let you see the output page by page).

Let's assume that you have a long directory listing. (If you want to try this example and need a directory with lots of files, use cd first to change to a system directory such as */bin* or */usr/bin*.) To make it easier to read the sorted listing, pipe the output through less:

```
$ cd /bin
$ ls -l | sort +4n | less
total 8288
-r-xr-xr-x  1 root  wheel     9736 27 Aug 04:36 echo
-r-xr-xr-x  1 root  wheel    10256 27 Aug 04:44 sync
-r-xr-xr-x  1 root  wheel    10476 27 Aug 05:03 domainname
...
-r-sr-xr-x  1 root  wheel    25248 27 Aug 05:03 rcp
-r-xr-xr-x  1 root  wheel    27308 27 Aug 04:31 dd
```

less reads a screenful of text from the pipe (consisting of lines sorted by order of file size), then prints a colon (:) prompt. At the prompt, you can type a less command to move through the sorted text. less reads more text from the pipe, shows it to you, and saves a copy of what it has read, so you can go backward to reread previous text if you want. (The simpler pager program more can't back up while reading from a pipe.) When you're done seeing the sorted text, the q command quits less.

Exercise: Redirecting Input/Output

In the following exercises, you redirect output, create a simple pipe, and use filters to modify output:

Task	Command
Redirect output to a file.	`ls > files`
Change all the letters to uppercase.	`tr '[a-z]' '[A-Z]' < files`
Sort the output of a program.	`ls	sort`
Append sorted output to a file.	`ls	sort >> files`
Display output to the screen.	`less files (or more files)`
Display long output to the screen.	`ls -l /bin	less (or more)`
Format and print a file with `pr`.	`pr files	lp or pr files	lpr`

## CHAPTER 7

Multitasking

Mac OS X can do many jobs at once, dividing the processor's time between the tasks so quickly that it looks as if everything is running at the same time. This is called *multitasking*.

With a window system, you can have many applications running at the same time, with many windows open. But Mac OS X, like most Unix systems, also lets you run more than one program inside the same Terminal. This is called *job control*. It gives some of the benefits of window systems to users who don't have windows. But, even if you're using a window system, you may want to use job control to do several things inside the same Terminal window. For instance, you may prefer to do most of your work from one Terminal window, instead of covering your desktop with multiple windows.

Why else would you want job control? Suppose you're running a program that will take a long time to process. On a single-task operating system, you would enter the command and wait for the system prompt to return, telling you that you could enter a new command. In Mac OS X, however, you can enter new commands in the "foreground" while one or more programs are still running in the "background."

When you enter a command as a background process, the shell prompt reappears immediately so that you can enter a new command. The original program will still run in the background, but you can use the system to do other things during that time. Depending on your system and your shell, you may even be able to log off and let the background process run to completion.

Running a Command in the Background

Running a program as a background process is most often done to free a Terminal when you know the program will take a long time to run. It's also used whenever you want to launch a new application from an existing Terminal window—so that you can keep working in the existing Terminal, as well as within the new application.

To run a program in the background, add the & character at the end of the command line before you press the Return key. The shell then assigns and displays a process ID number for the program:

```
$ sort bigfile > bigfile.sort &
[1] 372
$
```

Sorting is a good example because it can take a while to sort huge files.

The process ID (PID) for this program is 372. The PID is useful when you want to check the status of a background process, or if you need to cancel it. To check on the status of the process, use ps -up *PID*; if you want to cancel a process, use kill *PID*. In this instance, these commands would look like:

```
$ ps -up 372
USER     PID %CPU %MEM    VSZ   RSS TT  STAT STARTED      TIME COMMAND
taylor   372  0.0  0.0  18208   340 std  S    10:56PM   0:00.04 sort
$ kill 372
$
```

Fortunately, you don't need to remember the PID every time, because there are Unix commands (explained in the next section) to check on the processes you have running. Also, bash writes a status line to your screen when the background process finishes.

In bash, you can put an entire sequence of commands separated by semicolons (;) into the background by putting an ampersand (&) at the end of the entire command line. In other shells, enclose the command sequence in parentheses before adding the ampersand:

```
(command1; command2) &
```

Mac OS X Unix shells also have a feature (mentioned earlier) called *job control*. You can use the *suspend character* (usually Control-Z) to suspend a program running in the foreground. The program pauses, and you get a new shell prompt. You can then do anything else you like, including putting the suspended program into the background using the bg command. The fg command brings a suspended or background process to the foreground.

For example, you might start sort running on a big file, and, after a minute, want to edit a file. Stop sort, then put it in the background. The shell prints a message, and then another shell prompt, at which you can enter your vi command while sort runs.

```
$ sort hugefile1 hugefile2 > sorted
...time goes by...
CTRL-Z
Stopped
$ bg
[1]    sort hugefile1 hugefile2 > sorted &
$ vi test.txt
```

Checking on a Process

If a background process takes too long, or you change your mind and want to stop a process, you can check the status of the process and even cancel it.

ps

When you enter the command ps, you can see how long a process has been running, the process ID of the background process, and the terminal from which it was run. The tty program shows the name of the Terminal where it's running; this is especially helpful when you're logged into multiple terminals, as the following code shows:

```
$ ps
  PID  TT  STAT     TIME COMMAND
  347 std  S       0:00.17 -bash
  391  p2  S+      0:00.02 -bash
$ tty
/dev/ttyp1
```

std corresponds to your current Terminal window, and p2 corresponds to the Terminal window for ttyp2. In its basic form, ps lists the following:

Process ID (PID)
   A unique number assigned by Unix to the process.

Terminal name (TT)
   The Unix name for the terminal from which the process was started.

Runtime state (STAT)
   The current state of each job. S is sleeping, R is runnable, T is stopped, and I is idle (sleeping for more than 20–30 seconds). Additionally, the state can include + to indicate it's part of the foreground group process, E to indicate the process is exiting, and W to mean it's swapped out.[*]

---

[*] The ps manpage has details on all possible states for a process. It's quite interesting reading.

Runtime (TIME)

The amount of computer time (in minutes and seconds) that the process has used.

COMMAND

The name of the process.

Each terminal window has its own terminal name. The previous code shows processes running on two windows: *std* and *p2*. If you want to see the processes that a certain user is running, type ps -U *username*, where *username* is the username of someone logged into the system.

To see all processes running on the system, use ps -ax. The -a option shows processes from all users, and the -x option shows processes that are not connected with a Terminal session; many of these are processes that are a core part of Mac OS X, while others may be graphical programs you are running, such as a web browser.

Indeed, you can find out what processes are being run as root by using grep and adding a –u flag to get user-oriented output (basically more fields):

```
$ ps -aux | grep root | head
root     408  3.0  0.0    18096   344 std  R+  11:06PM  0:00.02 ps -aux
root      87  0.0  0.1    27868  1036 ??   Ss  10:38PM  0:01.26 /usr/
sbin/diskarbitrationd
root      89  0.0  0.1    19220   804 ??   Ss  10:38PM  0:00.08 /usr/
sbin/notifyd
root     116  0.0  0.0    27472   328 ??   Ss  10:38PM  0:00.28 netinfod
-s local
root     118  0.0  0.0    18048   112 ??   Ss  10:38PM  0:00.40 update
root     121  0.0  0.0    18076   120 ??   Ss  10:38PM  0:00.00 dynamic_
pager -F /private/var/vm/swapf
root     139  0.0  0.8    34280  6404 ??   Ss  10:38PM  0:01.40 /System/
Library/CoreServices/coreservi
root     161  0.0  0.1    28884  1052 ??   Ss  10:38PM  0:00.18 /System/
Library/CoreServices/SecurityS
root     172  0.0  0.1    27744   648 ??   Ss  10:38PM  0:00.20 /usr/
sbin/distnoted
root     177  0.0  0.0    27608   184 ??   Ss  10:38PM  0:00.00 cron
```

This is particularly long, so if you want to be fancy, you can add one more command to the pipe to just see the running commands: the awk filtering tool:

```
$ ps -aux | grep root | awk '{ print $1,$2,$11 }' | head
root 118 update
root 84 kextd
root 86 /usr/sbin/configd
root 87 /usr/sbin/diskarbitrationd
root 89 /usr/sbin/notifyd
root 116 netinfod
```

```
root 121 dynamic_pager
root 139 /System/Library/CoreServices/coreservi
root 161 /System/Library/CoreServices/SecurityS
root 172 /usr/sbin/distnoted
$
```

This command specifies that we are only interested in the first, second, and eleventh fields in the input stream.

top

Another way to see what applications are running and which are taking up the most resources is to use the helpful top command. Figure 7-1 shows the top command in action.

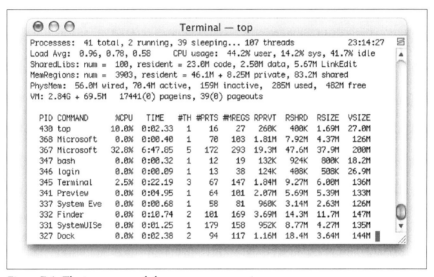

Figure 7-1. The top command shows processes running

If you're curious what commands consume the most system resources, leave top running in a Terminal window while you work. However, do be aware that the top command itself consumes some system resources, so if you're not paying attention to its output, type q to quit. You can always start it up again if things seem to be oddly slow on your computer.

top packs a lot of information into its display, considerably more than we have space to explain here. However, we do have one quick tip: to have processes shown sorted by CPU usage (rather than process ID), use top -o cpu to start the program. We recommend you look at man top for more information. Panther also comes with a very attractive top-like application worth exploring: *Applications/Utilities/Activity Monitor*.

Watching System Processes

ps -ax tells you what system processes are running, but if you want to see what they are up to, you'll need to look in the system log. To view the system log, use the command tail. It's kind of like cat, except that it prints only the last few lines of the file. If you use the -f option, it will follow the file as it grows. So, if you open up a new Terminal window and issue the following command, you can monitor the informational messages that come out of system utilities:

```
$ tail -f /var/log/system.log
Sep 24 22:38:45 localhost /usr/libexec/ConsoleMessage: Talking to
Directory Services
Sep 24 22:38:45 localhost /usr/libexec/ConsoleMessage: Getting Local
Users
Sep 24 22:38:47 localhost kernel: IP packet filtering initialized,
divert enabled, rule-based forwarding enabled, default to accept,
logging disabled
Sep 24 22:38:47 localhost kernel: IPv6 packet filtering initialized,
default to accept, logging disabled
Sep 24 22:38:47 localhost kernel: IP firewall loaded
```

When you're done, use Control-C to get a new command prompt. You can also see some system messages by running the Console application (*/Applications/ Utilities*).

You can also specify process ID values to ps to find out about specific jobs. Consider the following:

```
$ sort verybigfile > big-sorted-output
[1]  522
$ ps 522
  PID TT  STAT      TIME COMMAND
  522 std R      0:00.32 sort verybigfile
$ ps $$
  PID TT  STAT      TIME COMMAND
 347 std S      0:00.35 -bash
```

As the last command shows, you can easily ascertain what command shell you're running at any time by using the $$ shortcut for the process ID of the current shell. Feed $$ to ps, and it'll tell you which shell you're running.

You should be aware that there are two types of programs on Unix systems: *directly executable programs* and *interpreted programs*. Directly executable programs are written in a programming language such as C, and have been compiled into a binary format that the system can execute directly. Interpreted programs, such as shell and Perl scripts, are sequences of commands that are read by an interpreter program. If you execute an interpreted program, you will see an additional command (such as perl, sh, or csh) in the ps listing, as well as any Unix commands that the interpreter is executing currently.

Shells with job control have a command called jobs that lists background processes started from that shell. As mentioned earlier, there are commands to change the foreground/background status of jobs. There are other job control commands as well. See the references in the section "Documentation" in Chapter 10.

Canceling a Process

You may decide that you shouldn't have put a process in the background or the process is taking too long to execute. You can cancel a background process if you know its process ID.

> Mac OS X includes a very helpful utility called Force Quit, accessible from the Apple menu, which can be quite useful when applications are stuck or nonresponsive. However, commands entered into the Terminal window can only be cancelled from the command line—they don't show up in *Force Quit*. In addition, *Force Quit* doesn't show you administrative processes. To stop Unix programs and administrative processes, you must use the command line or the Activity Monitor.

kill

The kill command terminates a process. This has the same result as using the Finder's Force Quit command. The kill command's format is:

```
kill PID(s)
```

kill terminates the designated process IDs (shown under the PID heading in the ps listing). If you do not know the process ID, do a ps first to display the status of your processes.

In the following example, the sleep *n* command simply causes a process to "go to sleep" for *n* seconds. We enter two commands, sleep and who, on the same line, as a background process.

```
$ (sleep 60;who) &
[1] 472
$ ps
  PID TT  STAT      TIME COMMAND
  347 std S      0:00.36 -bash
  472 std S      0:00.00 -bash
  473 std S      0:00.01 sleep 60
$ kill 473
```

```
$ -bash: line 53:    473 Terminated              sleep 60
taylor   console  Sep 24 22:38
taylor   ttyp1    Sep 24 22:40

[1]+  Done                    ( sleep 60; who )
$
```

We decided that 60 seconds was too long to wait for the output of who. The
ps listing showed that sleep had the process ID number 473, so we use this
PID to kill the sleep process. You should see a message like "terminated" or
"killed"; if you don't, use another ps command to be sure the process has
been killed.

In our example, the who program is now executed immediately, as it is no
longer waiting on sleep; it lists the users logged into the system.

Problem checklist

The process didn't die when I told it to.

Some processes can be hard to kill. If a normal kill of these processes is
not working, enter kill -9 *PID*. This is a sure kill and can destroy almost
anything, including the shell that is interpreting it.

In addition, if you've run an interpreted program (such as a shell script),
you may not be able to kill all dependent processes by killing the interpreter process that got it all started; you may need to kill them individually. However, killing a process that is feeding data into a pipe generally
kills any processes receiving that data.

## CHAPTER 8

Accessing the Internet

A network lets computers communicate with each other, sharing files, email, and much more. Unix systems have been networked for more than 25 years, and Macintosh systems have always had networking as an integral part of the system design from the very first system released in 1984.

This chapter introduces Unix networking: remotely accessing your Mac from other computers and copying files between computers. It also shows you how the Connect to Server capability of Terminal can make common connections a breeze once you've set them up the first time.

Remote Logins

There may be times when you need to access your Mac, but you can't get to the desk it's sitting on. If you're working on a different computer, you may not have the time or inclination to stop what you're doing, walk over to your Mac, and log in (laziness may not be the only reason for this: perhaps someone else is using your Mac when you need to get on it or perhaps your Mac is miles away). Mac OS X's file sharing (System Preferences → Sharing) can let you access your files, but there may be times you want to use the computer interactively, perhaps to move files around, search for a particular file, or perform a system maintenance task.

If you enable Remote Login under System Preferences → Sharing, you can access your Mac's Unix shell from any networked computer that can run SSH (*http://www.ssh.com*), OpenSSH (*http://www.openssh.org*), or a compatible application such as PuTTY (a Windows implementation of SSH available at *http://www.chiark.greenend.org.uk/~sgtatham/putty/*). SSH and OpenSSH can be installed on many Unix systems, and OpenSSH is included with many Linux distributions, including Mac OS X.

Figure 8-1 shows how remote login programs such as ssh work. In a local login, you interact directly with the shell program running on your local system. In a remote login, you run a remote-access program on your local system; that program lets you interact with a shell program on the remote system.

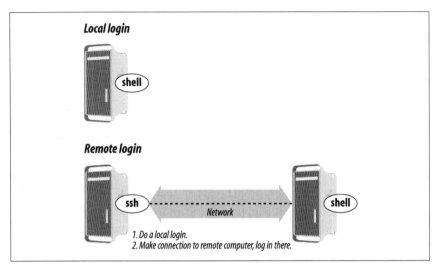

Figure 8-1. Local login, remote login

When you enable Remote Login, the Sharing panel will display instructions for logging into your Mac from another computer. This message is shown in Figure 8-2.

To log into your Mac from a remote Unix system, use the command displayed in the Sharing panel, as shown in the following sample session where a user on a Red Hat Linux system is connecting to a Mac OS X computer (the first time you connect, you'll be asked to vouch for your Mac's authenticity):

```
Red Hat: taylor $ ssh taylor@192.168.1.100
The authenticity of host '192.168.1.100 (192.168.1.100)' can't be
established.
RSA key fingerprint is 86:f6:96:f9:22:50:ea:4c:02:0c:58:a7:e4:a8:10:67.
Are you sure you want to continue connecting (yes/no)? yes
Warning: Permanently added '192.168.1.100' (RSA) to the list of known hosts.
taylor@192.168.1.100's password:
Last login: Thu Sep 25 10:27:58 2003
Welcome to Darwin!
~ 452 $
```

To log in to your Mac from a Windows machine using PuTTY, launch the PuTTY application, specify SSH (the default is to use the Telnet protocol

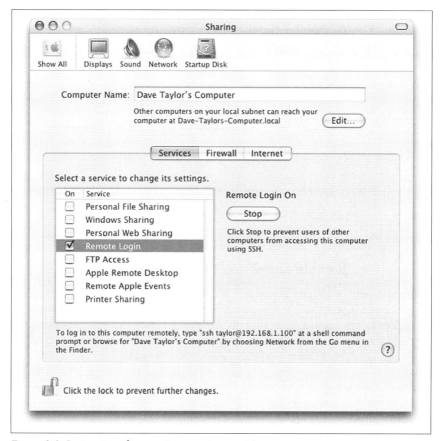

Figure 8-2. Instructions for remote access to your Mac

described later), and type in your Mac OS X system's IP address as shown in the Mac's Sharing panel. PuTTY will prompt you for your Mac OS X username and password. Figure 8-3 shows a sample PuTTY session.

Web and FTP Access

You can also use the Sharing preferences panel to enable your system's web and FTP server. Start Personal Web Sharing to enable the web server. Other users can access the main home page (located in */Library/WebServer/ Documents*) using *http://address*, where *address* is your machine's IP address or hostname (see the sidebar "Remote Access and the Outside World" if you are using an Airport Base Station or other router between your network and the Internet).

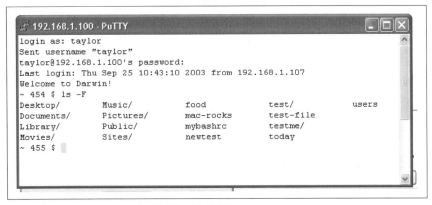

```
192.168.1.100 - PuTTY                                         _ □ ✕
login as: taylor
Sent username "taylor"
taylor@192.168.1.100's password:
Last login: Thu Sep 25 10:43:10 2003 from 192.168.1.107
Welcome to Darwin!
~ 454 $ ls -F
Desktop/        Music/          food            test/           users
Documents/      Pictures/       mac-rocks       test-file
Library/        Public/         mybashrc        testme/
Movies/         Sites/          newtest         today
~ 455 $
```

Figure 8-3. Connecting to Mac OS X with PuTTY

Remote Access and the Outside World

If your Macintosh has an IP address that was assigned by an AirPort Base Station, then it's very likely that your machine will not be visible to the outside world. Because of this, you will only be able to connect to your Mac from machines on your network. You can allow remote users to connect by using the AirPort Admin Utility → Show All Settings → Port Mapping (for Remote Login via ssh, you must map port 22 to your Macintosh; use port 80 for Personal Web Sharing). Other SoHo (Small Office/Home Office) gateways may support this feature as well.

If you use this technique, the IP address shown on the Sharing panel will be incorrect. You should use your AirPort Base Station's WAN address when you connect from a computer outside your network.

Start FTP Access to enable remote users to use FTP to connect to your system. Again, remote users should use your machine's IP address or hostname to connect.

Remote Access to Other Unix Systems

You can also connect to other systems from Mac OS X. To do so, launch the Terminal application. Then start a program that connects to the remote computer. In addition to ssh, some typical programs for connecting over a computer network are telnet, rsh (remote shell), or rlogin (remote login). All of these are supported and included with Mac OS X. In any case, when you log off the remote computer, the remote login program quits and you get another shell prompt from your Mac.

The syntax for most remote login programs is:

```
program-name remote-hostname
```

For example, when Dr. Nelson wants to connect to the remote computer named *biolab.medu.edu*, she'd first make a local login to her Mac named *fuzzy* by launching Terminal. Next, she'd use the telnet program to reach the remote computer. Her session would look something like this:

```
Welcome to Darwin!
~ 452 $ telnet biolab.medu.edu

Medical University Biology Laboratory

biolab.medu.edu login: jdnelson
Password:

biolab$
.
.
.
biolab$ exit
Connection closed by foreign host.
~ 453 $
```

Her accounts have shell prompts that include the hostname. This reminds her when she's logged in remotely. If you use more than one system but don't have the hostname in your prompt, see the sections "Changing Your Prompt" in Chapter 1 or ""Documentation" in Chapter 10 to find out how to add it.

 Actually, Dr. Nelson would be unwise to use telnet to connect to the remote system, because ssh is a much more secure alternative and is highly preferred. However, some remote sites still stick with telnet, and while it's important to encourage them to switch to ssh-only access, you will still sometimes find yourself using telnet, as shown here.

Also, when you're logged on to a remote system, keep in mind that the commands you type will take effect on the remote system, not your local one! For instance, if you use lpr to print a file, the printer it comes out of may be very far away.

The programs rsh (also called rlogin) and ssh generally don't give you a login: prompt. These programs assume that your remote username is the same as your local username. If they're different, give your remote username on the command line of the remote login program, as shown in the next example.

You may be able to log in without typing your remote password or pass-phrase.* Otherwise, you'll be prompted after entering the command line.

Following are four sample ssh and rsh command lines. The first pair shows how to log in to the remote system, *biolab.medu.edu*, when your username is the same on both the local and remote systems. The second pair shows how to log in if your remote username is different (in this case, *jdnelson*); note that the Mac OS X versions of ssh and rsh may support both syntaxes shown depending on how the remote host is configured:

```
$ ssh biolab.medu.edu
$ rsh biolab.medu.edu
$ ssh jdnelson@biolab.medu.edu
$ rsh -l jdnelson biolab.medu.edu
```

About Security

Today's Internet and other public networks have users who try to break into computers and snoop on other network users. While the popular media calls these people *hackers*, most hackers are self-respecting programmers who enjoy pushing the envelope of technology. The evildoers are better known as *crackers*. Most remote login programs (and file transfer programs, which we cover later in this chapter) were designed 20 years ago or more, when networks were friendly places with cooperative users. Those programs (many versions of telnet and rsh, for instance) make a cracker's job easy. They transmit your data, including your password, across the network in a way that allows even the most inexperienced crackers to read it. Worse, some of these utilities can be configured to allow access without passwords.

SSH is different; it was designed with security in mind. It sends your password (and everything else transmitted or received during your SSH session) in a secure way. A good place to get more details on SSH is the book *SSH: The Secure Shell*, by Daniel J. Barrett and Richard Silverman (O'Reilly).

Transferring Files

You may need to copy files between computers. For instance, you can put a backup copy of an important file you're editing onto an account at a computer in another building or another city. Or, Dr. Nelson could put a copy of a data file from her local computer onto a central computer, where her

---

* In ssh, you can run an *agent* program, such as ssh-agent, that asks for your passphrase once, then handles authentication every time you run ssh or scp afterward.

colleagues can access it. Or you might want to download 20 files from an FTP server, but not want to go through the tedious process of clicking on them one by one in a web browser window. If you need to do this sort of thing often, you may be able to set up a networked filesystem connection; then you'll be able to use the Finder or local programs such as cp and mv. But Unix systems also have command-line tools for transferring files between computers. These often work more quickly than graphical tools. We explore them later in this section.

scp and rcp

Mac OS X includes both scp (secure copy) and rcp (remote copy) programs for copying files between two computers. In general, you must have accounts on both computers to use these. The syntax of scp and rcp are similar to cp, but also let you add the remote hostname to the start of a file or directory pathname. The syntax of each argument is:

> *hostname:pathname*

hostname: is needed only for remote files. You can copy from a remote computer to the local computer, from the local computer to a remote computer, or between two remote computers.

The scp program is much more secure than rcp, so we suggest using scp to transfer private files over insecure networks such as the Internet. For privacy, scp encrypts the file and your passphrase.

For example, let's copy the files *report.may* and *report.june* from your home directory on the computer named *giraffe.intuitive.com* and put the copies into your working directory (.) on the machine you're presently logged in to. If you haven't set up the SSH agent that lets you use scp without typing your passphrase, scp will ask you:

```
$ scp giraffe.intuitive.com:report.may giraffe.intuitive.com:report.june .
Enter passphrase for RSA key 'taylor@mac':
```

To use wildcards in the remote filenames, put quotation marks ("*name*") around each remote name.* You can use absolute or relative pathnames; if you use relative pathnames, they start from your home directory on the remote system. For example, to copy all files from your *food/lunch* subdirectory on your *giraffe* account into your working directory (.) on the local account, enter:

```
$ scp "giraffe.intuitive.com:food/lunch/*" .
```

---

* Quotes tell the local shell not to interpret special characters, such as wildcards, in the filename. The wildcards are passed, unquoted, to the remote shell, which interprets them *there*.

Unlike cp, the Mac OS X versions of scp and rcp don't have an -i safety option. If the files you're copying already exist on the destination system (in the previous example, that's your local machine), those files are overwritten.

If your system has rcp, your system administrator may not want you to use it for system security reasons. Another program, ftp, is more flexible and secure than rcp (but much less secure than scp).

FTP

FTP, or file transfer protocol, is a standard way to transfer files between two computers. Many users of earlier Mac OS versions are familiar with Fetch (*http://fetchsoftworks.com/*), a shareware graphical FTP client that runs on Mac OS X as well as earlier versions.

The Unix ftp program does FTP transfers from the command line. There are also a number of easy-to-use graphical FTP tools available from the Apple web site (go to "Get Mac OS X Software…" from the Apple menu and click on Internet Utilities). But we cover the standard ftp program here. The computers on either end of the FTP connection must be connected by a network (such as the Internet).

To start FTP, identify yourself to the remote computer by giving the username and password for your account on that remote system. Unfortunately, sending your username and password over a public network means that snoopers might see them—and use them to log into your account on that system.

A special kind of FTP, *anonymous FTP*, happens if you log into the remote server with the username *anonymous*. The password is your email address, such as *alex@foo.co.uk*. (The password isn't usually required; it's a courtesy to the remote server.) Anonymous FTP lets anyone log into a remote system and download publicly accessible files to their local systems. Here's how that might look:

```
$ ftp ftp.apple.com
Trying 17.254.16.11...
Connected to ftp.apple.com.
220 ProFTPD 1.2.8 Server (Apple Anonymous FTP Server) [ftp02.apple.com]
Name (ftp.apple.com:taylor): ftp
331 Anonymous login ok, send your complete email address as your password.
Password:
230 Anonymous access granted, restrictions apply.
Remote system type is UNIX.
Using binary mode to transfer files.
ftp> dir
500 EPSV not understood
227 Entering Passive Mode (17,254,16,11,223,250).
```

```
150 Opening ASCII mode data connection for file list
drwxrwxrwx   3 ftpprod  ftpprod      102 May  7 19:11 Apple_Support_Area
drwxrwxr-x  20 ftpprod  ftpprod      680 Aug 28 22:07 developer
drwxrwxr-x  30 ftpprod  ftpprod     1020 Sep 15 13:44 emagic
drwxrwxr-x  10 ftpprod  ftpprod      340 Sep  3 16:23 filemaker
drwxrwxrwx  10 ftpprod  ftpprod      340 Apr  7 16:50 research
226 Transfer complete.
ftp> quit
221 Goodbye.
$
```

Command-line ftp

To start the standard Unix ftp program, provide the remote computer's hostname:

    ftp hostname

ftp prompts for your username and password on the remote computer. This is something like a remote login (see the section "Remote Logins," earlier in this chapter), but ftp doesn't start your usual shell. Instead, ftp prints its own prompt and uses a special set of commands for transferring files. Table 8-1 lists the most important ftp commands.

Table 8-1. Some ftp commands

Command	Description
put *filename*	Copies the file *filename* from your local computer to the remote computer. If you give a second argument, the remote copy will have that name.
mput *filenames*	Copies the named files (you can use wildcards) from the local computer to the remote computer.
get *filename*	Copies the file *filename* from the remote computer to your local computer. If you give a second argument, the local copy will have that name.
mget *filenames*	Copies the named files (you can use wildcards) from the remote computer to the local computer.
prompt	A "toggle" command that turns prompting on or off during transfers with the mget and mput commands. By default, mget and mput will prompt you "mget *filename*?" or "mput *filename*?" before transferring each file; you answer y or n each time. Typing prompt once, from an ftp> prompt, stops the prompting; all files will be transferred without question until the end of the ftp session. Or, if prompting is off, typing prompt at an ftp> prompt resumes prompting.
hash	Displays progress marks on file uploads and downloads so you can gauge progress. Particularly helpful with large transfers.
cd *pathname*	Changes the working directory on the remote machine to *pathname* (ftp typically starts at your home directory on the remote machine).

Table 8-1. Some ftp commands (continued)

Command	Description
lcd *pathname*	Changes ftp's working directory on the local machine to *pathname*. (ftp's first local working directory is the same working directory from which you started the program.) Note that the ftp lcd command changes only ftp's working directory. After you quit ftp, your shell's working directory will not have changed.
dir	Lists the remote directory (like ls -l).
binary	Tells ftp to copy the file(s) that follow it without translation. This preserves pictures, sound, or other data.
ascii	Transfers plain-text files, translating data if needed. For instance, during transfers between a Microsoft Windows system (which adds Control-M to the end of each line of text) and a Unix system (which doesn't), an ascii-mode transfer removes or adds those characters as needed.
passive	Toggles the setting of passive mode. This may help ftp to run correctly if you are behind a firewall. If you put the command setenv FTP_PASSIVE 1 in your *.tcshrc*, all your ftp sessions will use passive mode.
quit	Ends the ftp session and takes you back to a shell prompt.

Here's an example. Carol moves into the local directory she wants to use as a starting point (a good idea whether you're uploading or downloading), then uses ftp to copy the file *todo* from her *work* subdirectory on her account on the remote computer *rhino*:

```
$ cd uploads
$ ls
afile    ch2     somefile
$ ftp rhino.zoo.edu
Connected to rhino.zoo.edu.
Name (rhino:carol): csmith
Password:
ftp> cd work
ftp> dir
total 3
-rw-r--r--  1 csmith    mgmt    47 Feb  5  2001 for.ed
-rw-r--r--  1 csmith    mgmt   264 Oct 11 12:18 message
-rw-r--r--  1 csmith    mgmt   724 Nov 20 14:53 todo
ftp> get todo
local: todo remote: todo
227 Entering Passive Mode (17,254,16,11,224,18).
150 Opening BINARY mode data connection for todo (724 bytes)
226 Transfer complete.
724 bytes received in 00:00 (94.06 KB/s)
ftp> quit
$ ls
afile    ch2     somefile    todo
```

We've explored the most basic ftp commands here. Entering help at an ftp> prompt gives a list of all commands; entering help followed by an ftp command name gives a one-line summary of that command.

SFTP: FTP to secure sites

If you can only use `ssh` to connect to a remote site, chances are it won't support regular FTP transactions either, probably due to higher security. Mac OS X also includes a version of `ftp` that is compatible with the standard SSH server programs and works identically to regular FTP. Just type `sftp` at the command line. Here's an example:

```
$ cd downloads
$ sftp taylor@intuitive.com
Connecting to intuitive.com...
The authenticity of host 'intuitive.com (128.121.96.234)' can't be
established.
RSA key fingerprint is d0:db:8a:cb:74:c8:37:e4:9e:71:fc:7a:eb:d6:40:81.
Are you sure you want to continue connecting (yes/no)? yes
Warning: Permanently added 'intuitive.com,128.121.96.234' (RSA) to the list
of known hosts.
taylor@intuitive.com's password:
sftp> cd mybin
sftp> dir -l
drwxr-xr-x    0 24810     100          1024 Jun 26 20:18 .
drwxr-xr-x    0 24810     100          1536 Sep 16 18:59 ..
-rw-r--r--    0 24810     100           140 Jan 17  2003 .library.account.
info
-rwxr-xr-x    0 24810     100          3312 Jan 27  2003 addvirtual
...
-rw-r--r--    0 24810     100           406 Jan 24  2003 trimmailbox.sh
-rwxr-xr-x    0 24810     100          1841 Jan 24  2003 unpacker
-rwxr-xr-x    0 24810     100           946 Jan 22  2003 webspell
sftp> get webspell
webspell                       100%  946      4.7KB/s   00:00
sftp> quit
$ ls -l webspell
-rwxr-xr-x  1 taylor  taylor  946 25 Sep 11:28 webspell
```

FTP with a web browser

If you need a file from a remote site, and you don't need all the control that you get with the `ftp` program, you can use a web browser to download files using anonymous FTP. To do that, make a URL (location) with this syntax:

```
ftp://hostname/pathname
```

For instance, *ftp://somecorp.za/pub/reports/2001.pdf* specifies the file *2001.pdf* from the directory */pub/reports* on the host *somecorp.za*. In most cases, you can also start with just the first part of the URL—such as *ftp://somecorp.za*— and browse your way through the FTP directory tree to find what you want. If your web browser doesn't prompt you to save a file, use its Save menu command.

If you are using the Safari browser, it will open *ftp*: directories by mounting them in the Finder.

An even faster way to download a file is with the curl (copy from URL) command. For example, to save a copy of the report in the current directory, simply enter:

```
$ curl -O ftp://somecorp.za/pub/reports/2001.pdf
```

Without the -O option, curl will display the file in the Terminal window. If you want to read a text file from an Internet server, you can combine curl and less:

```
$ curl ftp://ftp.oreilly.com/pub/README.ftp | less
```

You can also use curl with web pages, but this will bring the page up in HTML source view:

```
$ curl http://www.oreilly.com | less
```

Other FTP solutions

One of the pleasures of working with Unix within the Mac OS X environment is that there are a wealth of great Aqua applications. In the world of FTP-based file transfer, the choices are all uniformly excellent, starting with *Fetch*, *NetFinder*, *Transmit*, *FTPeel*, *rbrowser*, and *Anarchie*, and encompassing many other possibilities. Either open the Apple menu and select "Get Mac OS X Software…", or try VersionTracker (see *http://www.versiontracker.com/*), Mac OS X Apps (see *http://www.macosxapps.com/*), MacUpdate (see *http:// macupdate.com/*), or the shareware archive site Download.com (see *http:// www.download.com/*).

Easy Shortcuts with Connect to Server

The Terminal application has a very helpful feature that can make connecting to remote systems via telnet, ssh, ftp, or sftp a breeze, once it's set up. Connect To Server is available off the File menu and is shown in Figure 8-4.

To add a service, click on the + icon on the left side of the window. More commonly, you'll add servers, which you can do by clicking on the + icon on the right side of the window. It produces a window that asks for the hostname or host IP address, which is easily entered, as shown in Figure 8-5.

Once added in one area, the new server is available for all services, so to connect to Apple's anonymous FTP archive site, choose ftp, then the new server name, and then enter **ftp** into the User box, as shown in Figure 8-6.

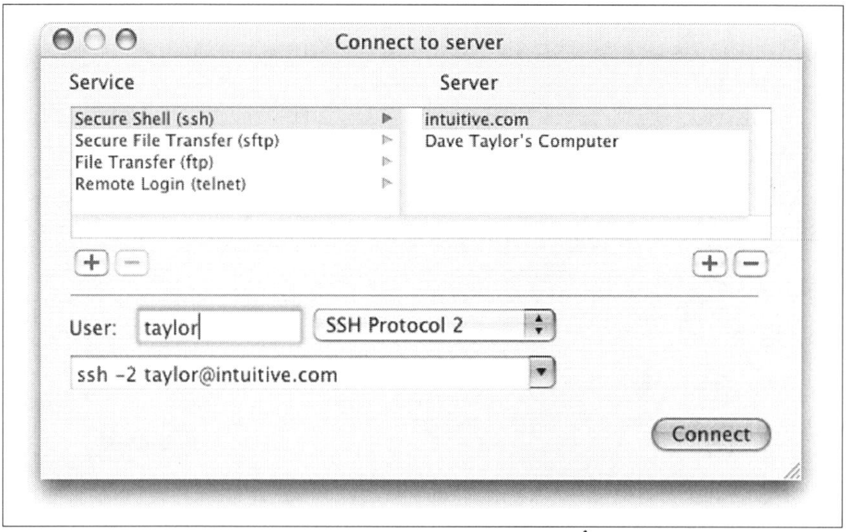

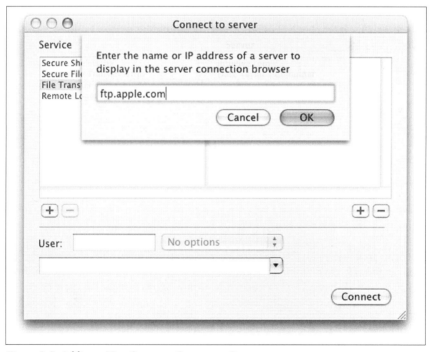

Figure 8-4. Connect to Server offers simple shortcuts

Figure 8-5. Adding a New Server to Connect to Server

Finally, the connection to Apple's server is a breeze: specify the server, specify the user, and click on Connect. The results are shown in Figure 8-7.

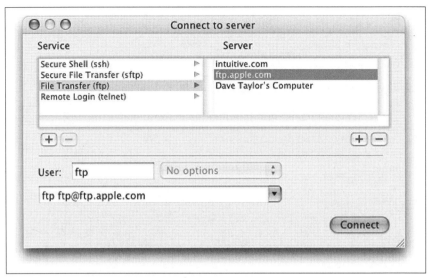

Figure 8-6. Specifying user ftp on ftp connections to ftp.apple.com

Figure 8-7. Instant connection to Apple's ftp server

Practice

You can practice your ftp skills by connecting to the public FTP archive *ftp. apple.com*. Log in as *ftp* with your email address as the password, then look around. Try downloading a research paper or document. If you have an account on a remote system, try using rcp and scp to copy files back and forth.

## CHAPTER 9

Of Windows and Downloads

Mac OS X comes with great applications, and a trip to the Apple Store or VersionTracker (*http://www.versiontracker.com/*) can bag you quite a few more. But there's a flood of new applications coming to your Mac OS X system because of its Unix core. Many of these are applications that have been around for a long time, and many are flowing in from other members of the Unix family, including Linux and FreeBSD. X11 is a terrific example: it's a graphical interface for Unix that's been around a long, long, time. Although the Mac OS X user interface is fantastic, there are many powerful Unix programs that require X11, but Apple's on top of it: Mac OS X 10.3 (Panther) includes X11 in the distribution. Read on to learn more about how you can use X11 on Mac OS X.

For typical Mac applications, freeware, shareware, or commercial, they're a breeze to install, thanks to the Mac OS X Installer. Unix applications don't have the same easy interface, but a team of dedicated programmers have created the next best thing, a powerful software distribution and installation system called Fink. Later in this chapter, we'll look at Fink, a project that makes it easy to add a vast amount of open source software to Mac OS X.

X11

The X Window System (commonly called X11 for short, reflecting that the current version is 11), is the standard graphical user interface for Unix systems. Mac OS X is a significant exception, as was its predecessor, NeXTStep. On Mac OS X, the Quartz Compositor is responsible for drawing what appears on your screen. In an X11-based system, an application called an *X server* handles this. The programs that run under X11, such as office applications, web browsers, and terminal windows, are X *clients*. X servers and clients talk to each other using Unix networking: if an X11 word processor needs to pop up a dialog asking whether you want to save a document, it makes a network connection to the X server and asks it to draw that window. Because X11 is networked in this way, you can run an X client on a machine across the office or across the planet, and have it display on your computer's X server.

X servers are typically full-screen applications that completely take over the display. Figure 9-1 shows a fullscreen X server running on a Linux computer. Three applications are running: an xterm (which is similar to the Mac OS X Terminal), a meter that shows how busy the Linux computer's CPU is, and a similar meter that's running on a Solaris system nearly one hundred miles away, measuring the system load on that box. In addition, a menu is visible. This belongs to the *window manager*, an X11 program that takes care of putting frames and window controls (such as close, resize, and zoom) around application windows. The window manager provides the overall look and feel, and also lets you launch applications and log out of X11. X11 users have many windows managers to choose from; the one shown in Figure 9-1 is *icewm*.

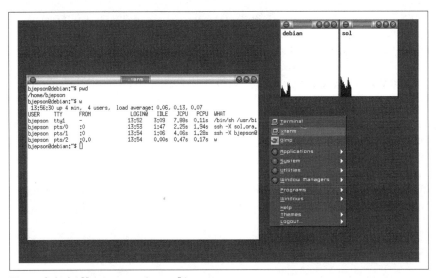

Figure 9-1. An X server running on Linux

Because X11 behaves very differently from Quartz, Apple's solution was to ship a *rootless* X server, which is an X server that does not take over the screen. Apple's X11 implementation, which includes the X server, many common X clients, and a software development kit for writing X11 applications, is derived from XFree86 (*http://www.xfree86.org*), the X11 release used on Linux, FreeBSD, NetBSD, OpenBSD, and many other operating systems.

Apple also created an X11 window manager, *quartz-wm*, which draws X11 windows that look and behave much like Quartz windows. As you can see, the X11 xterm and Mac OS X Terminal shown in Figure 9-2 look remarkably similar.

Figure 9-2. Examining an xterm and Mac OS X Terminal side by side

Installing X11

Apple's X11 is included with Mac OS X 10.3 Panther, but it is not installed by default. To locate the X11 installer, use the Finder to look for a file named *X11User.pkg* on the Mac OS X installation CD-ROMs. If you are using an earlier version of Mac OS X, or if you have trouble finding this file, visit *http://www.apple.com/macosx/x11/* for the latest information.

Double-click the Mac OS X installer to start it, and install it on your Mac, following the prompts. When the installer is finished, you'll have an application called *X11* in */Applications/Utilities*.

Using X11

Launch the X11 application by opening */Applications/Utilities* in the Finder and double-clicking on the X11 icon. After a few seconds, an xterm window will appear. You can start a new xterm by selecting File → New Window (or using ⌘-N). Click the Applications menu to see a list of shortcuts. By default, there are options for Terminal (starts a new xterm), xman (lets you browse Unix manpages), and xclock (displays a clock on the screen). Figure 9-3 shows X11 running along with these three applications.

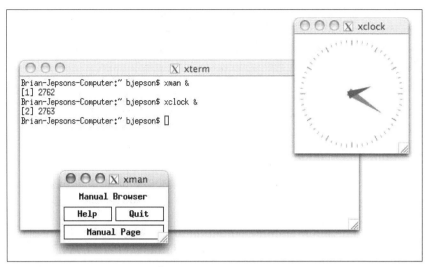

Figure 9-3. Running some X11 clients

X11 includes many other applications. To see a list, examine the X11 application directory with the command `ls /usr/X11R6/bin`. Here are a few of the most interesting utilities included with Mac OS X:

bitmap
An X11 bitmap (*.xbm*) editor.

glxgears
An OpenGL 3D graphics demonstration. OpenGL applications running under Apple's X11 implementation have the benefit of full 3D hardware acceleration.

glxinfo
Displays information about OpenGL capabilities.

oclock
An X11 clock.

xcalc
A calculator program that runs under X11.

xeyes
A pair of eyeballs that follows your mouse cursor.

xhost
Gives another computer permission to open windows on your display.

xkill
Changes your cursor to the "cursor of doom." Any X11 window you click in will be shut down. If you change your mind and don't want to kill an app, press Control-C. This will not kill any Aqua application; it works only on X11 applications.

xload

Displays the CPU load.

There are some significant differences between X11 and the Mac OS X interface that you need to watch out for. Although Apple's X11 does a great job of minimizing these differences, there are still some quirks that may throw you off:

Cutting and pasting

If you press ⌘-C while you've selected something in an X11 window, you can paste it into another Mac OS X application. But that's where the similarity ends: to paste something into an X11 window, you can't use ⌘-V. Instead, use Option-Click. If you have a three-button mouse, press the middle button to paste into an X11 window.

X11 application menus

The menu at the top of the screen always belongs to X11 itself. Individual X11 applications may have their own menu near the top of their main window. Figure 9-4 shows two different types of X11 application menus, a classic X11 menu from xmh (X11 mail reader) and a more modern X11 menu from gataxx (a game from the GNOME desktop system).

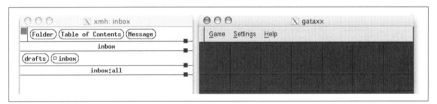

Figure 9-4. Comparing X11 menu styles

Be careful with ⌘-Q

If you press ⌘-Q (quit) while running an X11 application, this will attempt to shut down all of X11. Because of this, you'll get a warning if you try to do this when there are X11 clients running. Look for a quit option on the X11 application's own menu, or click the close button on its window.

Scrolling the xterm

By default, the xterm doesn't have scrollbars. However, like the Terminal, you can use a keystroke to scroll up and down, though, unfortunately, it's not the same keystroke: Terminal uses Page Up and Page Down, while xterm expects Shift-Page Up and Shift-Page Down.

Launching applications from the xterm

When you type the name of an X11 program in the xterm, it will launch, but the xterm window will appear to hang because it is waiting for the program to exit. To avoid this problem, you can either append the & character after the program name (to put it in the background) or press Control-Z after the program starts, and type **bg** to put the program in the background. See Figure 9-5 for an example of launching xeyes both ways.

 You can also use the *open-x11* command from within an xterm or the Mac OS X Terminal to launch an X11 application, as in open-x11 xterm.

X11, .bashrc, and .profile

If you've customized your Unix shell by editing *~/.profile*, applications that run under X11, including xterm, won't respect the settings in that file. To correct this problem, put any essential settings in your *~/.bashrc* file, which X11 will read. For more information, see the Apple X11 FAQ, which you can find by searching for "X11 FAQ" at *http://developer.apple.com/qa/*.

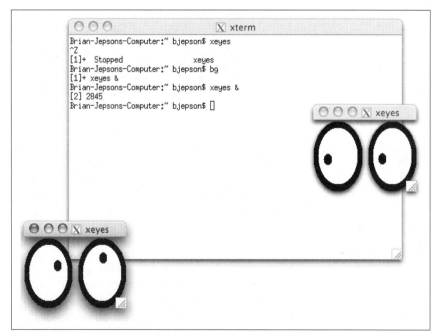

Figure 9-5. Launching X11 applications from the xterm

Customizing the Applications Menu

You can customize X11's Applications menu by selecting Applications → Customize. Click Add Item to insert a new item. Specify the menu title in the Name column, and use the Command column for the command to execute. You can also add any necessary parameters or switches here. For example, to change the Terminal/xterm menu item so it uses a 12-point antialiased Monaco font, add the switches -fa Monaco -fs 12, as shown in Figure 9-6.

 Although the Application Menu item for xterm is named Terminal, it's not the same as the Mac OS X Terminal application.

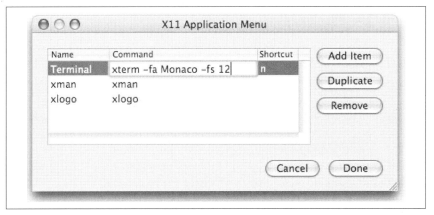

Figure 9-6. Configuring xterm to launch with a different font

You can also specify a shortcut in the shortcut column. The shortcut key must be used with the Command (⌘) key, so the n in the Terminal/xterm entry specifies the ⌘-N keystroke.

OpenOffice.org

OpenOffice.org is a free office suite that stands up remarkably well in a head-to-head comparison to Microsoft Office. It started life as StarOffice, and its owner, Sun Microsystems, continues to market it under that brand name (*http://www.sun.com/staroffice*). However, Sun has released the source code to most of StarOffice, and from that massive collection of source, the OpenOffice.org project was born.

OpenOffice.org is available in Windows and Unix (X11) versions. As of this writing, it does not have native support for Mac OS X. So, if you want to use this suite on Mac OS X, you'll need to run it under X11. However, an effort is underway to make OpenOffice.org a full-fledged Aqua application (see *http://porting.openoffice.org/mac/timeline.html*).

To install OpenOffice.org on your Mac:

1. Download the installer (*http://porting.openoffice.org/mac/*) for Open-Office.org. It is quite large (over 100 MB), so be patient.

2. Double-click the installer and follow the prompts. You will need to accept the license terms, consult a README file, and select installation options (the default selections are fine). The OpenOffice.org installer launches a couple of other installers, each of which will ask you for your password. During the installation, you may get a warning that "XDar-win does not exist in the Applications directory." This tells you that OpenOffice.org could not find the X11 installation it expected to find (XDarwin is another distribution of X11 for Mac OS X). However, OpenOffice.org will work fine with Apple's X11.

After you've installed OpenOffice.org, you can launch it by double-clicking *Start OpenOffice.org*, which is located in */Applications/OpenOffice.org1.0.3* (the last few numbers of that folder name may vary depending on which version of OpenOffice.org you have). The first time you launch this program, you'll be asked for the location of your X11 installation. Click Browse and select */Applications/Utilities/X11*. The OpenOffice.org word processor will appear, and you can select File → Open to open an existing document, or start typing to create a new one. Figure 9-7 shows the Microsoft Word document for the text of this chapter. Select File → New to create a spreadsheet, drawing, or presentation application.

You can also launch OpenOffice.org from within an xterm or Terminal with the following command:

```
open-x11 /Applications/OpenOffice.org1.0.3/program/soffice
```

Although OpenOffice.org does not use the full power of Mac OS X's Aqua GUI, it's one of the snazzier X11 applications out there. Also, it offers near-complete compatibility with Microsoft's Word, Excel, and PowerPoint. So although it's not perfect, the price is right, and it may be just what you need if you have to work with Microsoft Office formats but don't want to pur-chase the product.

Remote X11 Access to Your Mac

If you use other Unix systems that run X11, you can log in remotely to your Mac, run X11 applications, and have them display on that Unix system (the

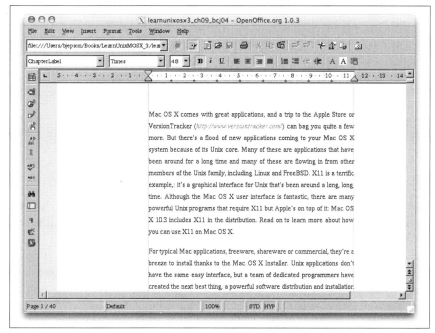

Mac OS X comes with great applications, and a trip to the Apple Store or VersionTracker (*http://www.versiontracker.com/*) can bag you quite a few more. But there's a flood of new applications coming to your Mac OS X system because of its Unix core. Many of these are applications that have been around for a long time and many of these are flowing in from other members of the Unix family, including Linux and FreeBSD. X11 is a terrific example,: it's a graphical interface for Unix that's been around a long, long time. Although the Mac OS X user interface is fantastic, there are many powerful Unix programs that require X11 but Apple's on top of it: Mac OS X 10.3 includes X11 in the distribution. Read on to learn more about how you can use X11 on Mac OS X.

For typical Mac applications, freeware, shareware or commercial, they're a breeze to install thanks to the Mac OS X Installer. Unix applications don't have the same easy interface, but a team of dedicated programmers have created the next best thing, a powerful software distribution and installation.

Figure 9-7. Editing a Microsoft Word document in OpenOffice.org.

applications are still executing on the Mac, but they appear on the Unix system). If you have an always-on broadband connection, you can even do this from afar (perhaps you use a Unix system at school or at work, but want to connect to your Mac at home).

These instructions apply only to X11 applications that are installed on your Mac. If you want a complete remote desktop solution, see Share My Desktop (*http://www.bombich.com/software/smd.html*). You'll be able to remotely control your Mac from any system for which you can get a VNC (Virtual Network Computer) client, including Windows, Unix, Palm, Pocket PC, cell phones, and more. See *http://www.realvnc.com/* for more information about VNC.

To set up your Mac for remote X11 access:

1. Use the command `sudo cp /etc/sshd_config /etc/sshd_config.backup` to make a backup of the configuration file you'll edit in the next step. If anything goes wrong during this process, you can use the command `sudo cp /etc/sshd_config.backup /etc/sshd_config` to restore the original file and restart your Mac.

2. Use the command `sudo vi /etc/sshd_config` to edit your remote login configuration file. Find the line that reads `#X11Forwarding no`. The leading # tells `sshd` to ignore that line in the file, and to use the default value instead. To be absolutely sure that remote X11 access is enabled, regardless of the default, remove the comment character (the "#"), and change no to yes. So, change this line to read `X11Forwarding yes`, and save the file.

3. Open System Preferences → Sharing and find the Remote Login setting. If it's disabled, enable it. If it's enabled, stop it and start it again to be sure that the configuration change you made in the previous step takes effect.

Pay attention to the instructions at the bottom of the Sharing preference pane (you need to have Remote Login selected for these to appear). This will tell you how to connect to your computer remotely. In Figure 9-8, it specifies the command `ssh bjepson@192.168.254.104` for connecting to Brian's computer. This command (with some changes; you'll have a different user name and IP address) will let you run X11 applications on your Mac and display them on other Mac OS X systems on the same network as your Mac. It will also work with any Unix system on the same network as your Mac that has either the commercial version of SSH from SSH Communications Security (*http://www.ssh.com/*) or the open source version (the version that Mac OS X uses) from *http://www.openssh.org/*.

To run X11 applications on your Mac and display them on another computer, take the following steps:

1. Log in to the remote machine. If it's a Mac, start X11 and bring the xterm window to the front or launch a new xterm from the Applications menu. If it's a Unix or Linux system, start X11 (many systems start it automatically), and open an xterm or other terminal application, such as dtterm.

2. On the remote machine, use `ssh +x` *hostname* (SSH Communications Security) or `ssh -X` *hostname* (OpenSSH) to connect to your Macintosh.

3. After you've logged in to your Mac over SSH, run the X11 application that you're interested in.

Figure 9-9 shows an example of connecting from a Solaris system and launching OpenOffice on the Macintosh (but it appears on the Solaris system instead of the Macintosh).

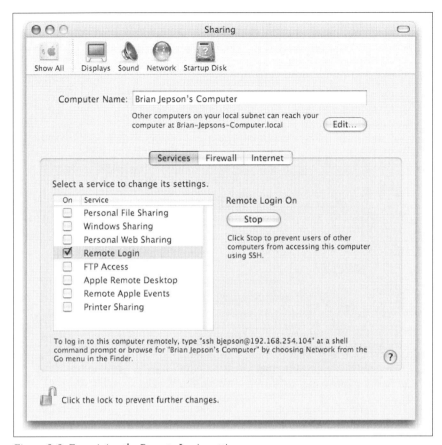

Figure 9-8. Examining the Remote Login settings

Opening a private network

If your Macintosh is on a private network and you try to connect from the outside, the command shown in the Sharing pane will probably fail, since private network addresses are not reachable from other networks on the Internet. If you use an AirPort base station or a non-Apple access point or router to connect your home network to a broadband connection, then you are almost certainly on a private network. However, you can use the Port Mapping tab of the AirPort Admin Utility (located in */Applications/Utilities*) to open a connection on port 22 (the port that SSH uses) and forward it to your Mac.

When you issue the ssh command from a remote machine, you'll need to replace the IP address shown in Sharing preferences to that of your AirPort base station (see the Internet tab of the Airport Admin Utility). Even with

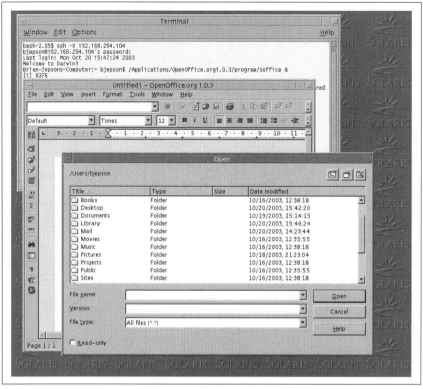

Figure 9-9. OpenOffice.org running on a Mac, but displayed on a Solaris system using remote X11

this configuration, remote access may not work, since some Internet Service Providers (ISPs) place restrictions on inbound connections.

X11 Access to Other Computers

You can also run X11 applications on other computers and display them on your Mac once you have X11 running. To do this:

1. Log in to your Mac, start X11 (Applications → Utilities → X11), and launch an xterm.

2. Issue the command `ssh -X` *hostname*, where *hostname* is the name or IP address of the remote computer.

3. After you've logged in to the remote machine, run the X11 application that you're interested in. Figure 9-10 shows Netscape running on a Solaris system, but displayed on a Macintosh via X11.

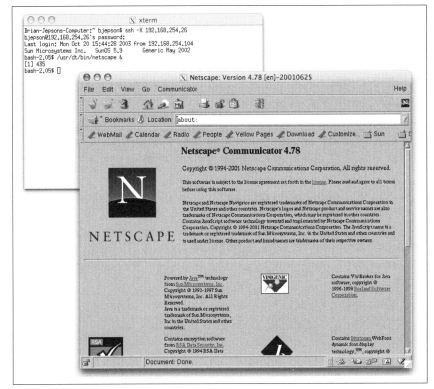

Figure 9-10. Running an application on Solaris, but displaying it on a Mac

Fink

The Fink Project is a mechanism for obtaining, installing, and keeping up-to-date a wide variety of open source applications on your Macintosh. The project itself is made up of volunteers who are dedicated to bringing the best open source software to Mac OS X. They fine-tune these open source applications for the Mac OS X environment, and then keep the applications updated so they work with the latest release of Mac OS X.

Many of the programs featured in this chapter are available through Fink, as is a wealth of other applications. To install Fink, do the following:

1. Download the Fink binary installer disk image (a *.dmg* file) from *http://fink.sourceforge.net/download*.

2. If your web browser doesn't automatically open the disk image, switch to the Finder and double-click the *.dmg* file to mount the disk image.

3. Open the mounted disk image and double-click the Fink Installer *.pkg* package inside.

4. Follow the instructions on the screen.

 You can also find an installer for many open source applications by selecting the "Get Mac OS X Software…" menu from the Apple menu, which opens a web browser and takes you to the Apple web site. From there, find and click on the "Unix & Open Source" link, which offers a list of useful Unix applications. The advantage of using Fink is that it will manage thousands of available packages, making sure that you have the latest versions and that different packages cooperate with each other.

To begin using Fink, you need to set up your PATH and some environment variables. Fortunately, Fink provides a shell script to help with this. Add this command to the end of your *.profile* file (see "The vi Text Editor" in Chapter 4):

```
. /sw/bin/init.sh
```

Next, close your Terminal window and open a new one. You won't notice anything different, but the addition to your *.profile* will configure future Terminal sessions for Fink. After you've installed Fink and started a new Terminal session, you can use the apt-get utility to install packages. When you issue the apt-get command, you must use sudo (see "Superuser Privileges with sudo" in Chapter 3) so you can make changes to the system.

After you've done a fresh install of Fink, your first step should always be to update the list of available packages with apt-get update (you can also run this command every couple of weeks to see whether any new packages have been released, perhaps by adding it to the cron *monthly* file):

```
$ sudo apt-get update
Password: ********
Get:1 http://us.dl.sourceforge.net release/main Packages [112kB]
Get:2 http://us.dl.sourceforge.net release/main Release [85B]
Get:3 http://us.dl.sourceforge.net release/crypto Packages [9247B]
Get:4 http://us.dl.sourceforge.net release/crypto Release [87B]
Get:5 http://us.dl.sourceforge.net current/main Packages [112kB]
Get:6 http://us.dl.sourceforge.net current/main Release [85B]
Get:7 http://us.dl.sourceforge.net current/crypto Packages [9247B]
Get:8 http://us.dl.sourceforge.net current/crypto Release [87B]
Fetched 243kB in 1s (207kB/s)
Reading Package Lists... Done
Building Dependency Tree... Done
```

Listing Available Packages

To see a list of available packages, use the command `fink list` (this sample shows an abbreviated list):

```
$ fink list | more
Information about 1710 packages read in 1 seconds.

        3dpong         0.4-2        Pong clone
        a2ps           4.12-4       Any to PostScript filter
  i     aalib          1.4rc5-2     Ascii art library
  i     aalib-bin      1.4rc5-2     Ascii art library
  i     aalib-shlibs   1.4rc5-2     Ascii art library
        abiword        1.0.2-2      Open-source word processor
[... output deleted for brevity...]
```

An `i` in the leftmost column indicates that the package is already installed. The second column is the package name. The third column shows the version number, and the last column provides a brief description of the package.

Installing Packages

You can use the `apt-get install` command to install a package, such as Lynx, a text-only web browser:

```
$ sudo apt-get install lynx
Reading Package Lists... Done
Building Dependency Tree... Done
The following NEW packages will be installed:
  lynx
0 packages upgraded, 1 newly installed, 0 to remove and 0  not upgraded.
Need to get 1319kB of archives. After unpacking 0B will be used.
Get:1 http://us.dl.sourceforge.net release/main lynx 2.8.4-1 [1319kB]
Fetched 1319kB in 11s (120kB/s)
Selecting previously deselected package lynx.
(Reading database ... 3450 files and directories currently installed.)
Unpacking lynx (from .../lynx_2.8.4-1_darwin-powerpc.deb) ...
Setting up lynx (2.8.4-1) ...
```

The web site *http://finkcommander.sourceforge.net/* is home to FinkCommander, a free graphical user interface for Fink. Use this program if you'd rather have a GUI interface to maintain your Fink installation.

When you use apt-get to install a package, Fink searches the Fink archive web site for a pre-built package provided by the volunteer team. A pre-built package is an application that has been bundled up in a manner similar to the installers used by other Mac OS X applications. Although the `fink list` command will list many packages, not all of them have binary packages. However, if you've installed the Mac OS X Xcode Tools, you can use the fink install command to automatically download, compile, and install an application. For example, as of this writing, there was no binary package for the command-line email program Pine. Here's how you'd install it using fink install:

```
$ fink install pine
sudo /sw/bin/fink  install pine
Password: ********
Information about 1710 packages read in 3 seconds.

pkg pine  version ###
pkg pine  version 4.44-2
The following package will be installed or updated:
 pine
[... output deleted for brevity...]
```

The fink install command performs a lot of actions on your behalf: downloading source code, locating patches (modifications to the source code that provide Mac OS X compatibility), compiling the source, and installing the compiled programs. This process can take a long time, depending on which packages you have selected. If you select a package that depends on another package, fink will automatically install them both. If there are many dependencies between packages, you could be in for a long wait.

For this reason, it's best to use apt-get to install packages whenever possible. Since apt-get uses precompiled packages, you don't have to download all the source and wait for compilation. Also, apt-get warns you if there are any dependencies, and gives you a chance to cancel the installation prior to adding software you're not sure about:

```
$ sudo apt-get install ethereal
Password: ********
Reading Package Lists... Done
Building Dependency Tree... Done
The following extra packages will be installed:
  dlcompat glib glib-shlibs gtk+ gtk+-data gtk+-shlibs libpcap
  libpcap-shlibs system-xfree86 zlib
The following NEW packages will be installed:
  dlcompat ethereal glib glib-shlibs gtk+ gtk+-data gtk+-shlibs
  libpcap libpcap-shlibs system-xfree86 zlib
0 packages upgraded, 11 newly installed, 0 to remove and 0  not upgraded.
Need to get 13.7MB of archives. After unpacking OB will be used.
Do you want to continue? [Y/n]
```

Some Picks

This section describes just a few of the applications you can install using Fink. First up is lynx, a text-based web browser that's great for viewing or downloading web pages quickly. After that, we talk about Pine, an email client and USENET newsreader. Finally, we discuss GIMP, a general-purpose graphics manipulation package that can do all sorts of great things with images.

Browsing the Web with Lynx

There are a number of excellent web browsers available for Mac OS X, including Safari, Camino, Mozilla, and OmniWeb. However, attractive, graphically based web browsers can be slow—especially with flashy, graphics-laden web pages on a slow network.

 To install Lynx, use the command `sudo apt-get install fink` (see "Installing Packages", earlier in this chapter).

The Lynx web browser (originally from the University of Kansas and available on many Unix systems) is different because it's a text-based web browser that works within the Terminal application. Being text-only causes it to have some trade-offs you should know about. Lynx indicates where graphics occur in a page layout; you won't see the graphics, but the bits of text that Lynx uses in their place can clutter the screen. Still, because it doesn't have to download or display those graphics, Lynx is *fast*, which is especially helpful over a dial-up modem or busy network connection. Sites with complex multicolumn layouts can be hard to follow with Lynx; a good rule is to page through the screens, looking for the link you want and ignore the rest. The Lynx command line syntax is:

```
lynx "location"
```

For example, to visit the O'Reilly home page, enter `lynx "http://www.oreilly.com"`, or simply `lynx "www.oreilly.com"`. Figure 9-11 shows part of the home page.

To move around the Web, use your keyboard's arrow keys, spacebar, and a set of single-letter commands. The third line from the bottom of a Lynx screen gives you a hint of what you might want to do at the moment. In Figure 9-11, for instance, "(NORMAL LINK) Use right-arrow or <return> to activate" means you can follow the link by pressing right arrow. The bottom two lines of the screen remind you of common commands, and the help system (which you get by typing h) lists the rest (use the spacebar to scroll forward one screenfull, and press b to move back a screenfull).

When you first view a screen, the link nearest the top is selected and highlighted. To select a later link (farther down the page), press the down-arrow

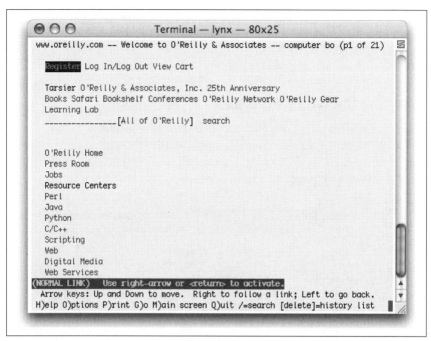

www.oreilly.com -- Welcome to O'Reilly & Associates -- computer bo (p1 of 21)

Register Log In/Log Out View Cart

Tarsier O'Reilly & Associates, Inc. 25th Anniversary
Books Safari Bookshelf Conferences O'Reilly Network O'Reilly Gear
Learning Lab
_____[All of O'Reilly] search

O'Reilly Home
Press Room
Jobs
Resource Centers
Perl
Java
Python
C/C++
Scripting
Web
Digital Media
Web Services
(NORMAL LINK)   Use right-arrow or <return> to activate.
Arrow keys: Up and Down to move. Right to follow a link; Left to go back.
H)elp O)ptions P)rint G)o M)ain screen Q)uit /=search [delete]=history list

Figure 9-11. Viewing the O'Reilly home page in Lynx

key. The up-arrow key selects the previous link (farther up the page). Once you've selected a link you want to visit, press the right-arrow key to follow that link; the new page appears. Go back to the previous page by pressing the left-arrow key (from any selected link; it doesn't matter which one).

Dumping a web page with Lynx

You can use Lynx to dump the contents of a web page in plain text, which you can then paste into an email message to send a web page around in a plain, easy-to-read format. Lynx preserves URLs in documents by formatting them as footnotes. To dump a web page, use lynx -dump *URL*, as in lynx -dump "http://www.intuitive.com/kana.shtml". This produces the following output:

```
Calligraphy
  "Chokkan"

    The calligraphy on the Intuitive Systems Web site was produced by
    Master Japanese Calligrapher [1]Eri Takase, and it means "insight" or
    "intuition":

      The first character means "direct". It is interesting in that it
      originally meant "ten eyes" or clear, transparent, no concealment.
```

The second character is constructed of characters meaning "bite the
heart" and now means "feel" or "sense".

Intuition means to "directly sense"

[2]close this window

References

1. http://www.takase.com/
2. javascript:window.close();

Electronic Mail with Pine

When you install Mac OS X or boot it for the first time, the installer may
ask whether you want to sign up for .Mac, Apple's suite of Internet services that includes *electronic mail* (email). If you signed up for .Mac, you
probably use Apple's Mail application to send and receive email. If you
didn't sign up for .Mac, you may be using an email account provided by
your ISP or employer along with Apple's Mail or some other application.

There are many great graphical mail applications for Mac OS X. However,
Terminal-based email programs have some benefits:

- They are not affected by conventional email viruses, although security
  holes do appear from time to time in nearly every program that inter-
  acts with the Internet.
- You can read your email while logged in to your Mac from another
  machine (see "Remote Logins" in Chapter 8).

Pine, from the University of Washington, is a popular program for reading
and sending email from a terminal. It works completely from your keyboard; you don't need a mouse.

Mac OS X does not include Pine by default. To install Pine, see "Installing
Packages," earlier in this chapter. Start Pine by entering its name at a shell
prompt. It also accepts options and arguments on its command line; to find
out more, enter pine -h (help). Figure 9-12 shows the starting display, i.e.,
the *main menu*.

Configuring Pine

The Pine main menu has a Setup entry for configuring Pine. After you enter
S (the "Setup" command), you can choose what kind of setup you want.
From the setup screen, you can get to the option configuration area with C
(the "Config" command).

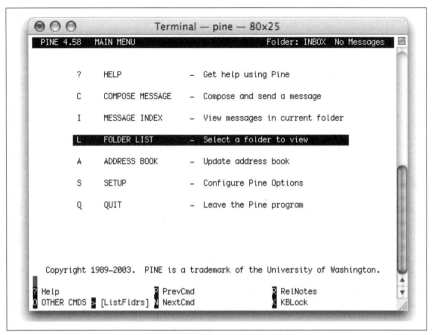

Figure 9-12. Pine main menu

The configuration screen has page after page of options. You can look through them with the spacebar (to move forward one page), the - key (back one page), the N key (to move forward to the next entry), and the P key (back to the previous entry). If you know the name of an option you want to change, you can search for it with W (the "Whereis" command).

When you highlight an option, the menu of commands at the bottom of the screen will show you what can do with that particular option. A good choice, while you're exploring, is the ? (help) command, to find out about the option you've highlighted. There are several kinds of options:

- Options with variable values: names of files, hostnames of computers, and so on. For example, the personal-name option sets the name used in the "From: " header field of mail messages you send. The setup entry looks like this:

  ```
  personal-name      = <No Value Set: using "Robert L. Stevenson">
  ```

  "No Value Set" can mean that Pine is using the default from the system-wide settings, as it is here. If this user wants his email to come from "Bob Stevenson," he could use the C (Change Val) command to set that name.

- Options that set preferences for various parts of Pine. For instance, the enable-sigdashes option in the "Composer Preferences" section puts two dashes and a space on the line before your default signature. The option line looks like this:

```
[X] enable-sigdashes
```

The X means that this preference is set, or "on." If you want to turn this option off, use the X (Set/Unset) command to toggle the setting.

- Options for which you can choose one of many possible settings. The option appears as a series of lines. For instance, the first few lines of the saved-msg-name-rule option look like this:

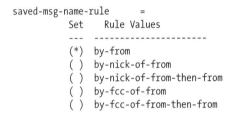

```
saved-msg-name-rule      =
             Set    Rule Values
             ---    ----------------------
             (*)   by-from
             ( )   by-nick-of-from
             ( )   by-nick-of-from-then-from
             ( )   by-fcc-of-from
             ( )   by-fcc-of-from-then-from
```

The * means that the saved-msg-name-rule option is currently set to by-from. (Messages will be saved to a folder named for the person who sent the message.) If you wanted to choose a different setting—for instance, by-fcc-of-from—you'd move the highlight to that line and use the * (Select) command to choose that setting.

These settings are trickier than the others, but the built-in help command ? explains each choice in detail. Start by highlighting the option name (here, saved-msg-name-rule) and reading its help info. Then look through the settings' names, highlight one you might want, and read its help info to see if it's right for you.

When you exit the setup screen with the E command, Pine asks you to confirm whether you want to save any option changes you made. Answer N if you were just experimenting or aren't sure.

Configuring Pine to send and receive email

Before you can send or receive email with Pine, you must configure it to talk to your email servers. You will need the following information (if you are not using .Mac, you will need to get this information from your ISP or system administrator):

Your email address
This will be supplied by your ISP. If you are using .Mac, it will be *username*@mac.com.

Your Mac OS X username must be the same as the username in your email address, since Pine uses your Mac OS X username and your *user-domain* to generate your email address.

Incoming mail server

> This is the server where your email messages sit until you're ready to read them. Your ISP may refer to this as a POP or IMAP server. If you are using .Mac, this will be `mail.mac.com`.

Incoming mail protocol

> Pine supports two protocols for downloading remote email: POP (Post Office Protocol) and IMAP (Internet Message Access Protocol). If you are using . Mac, this will be IMAP.

Outgoing mail server

> This is a server that accepts your outgoing email and delivers it to the recipients. Your ISP may refer to this as an SMTP server (SMTP is Simple Mail Transfer Protocol, the network protocol for sending and receiving email). If you are using .Mac, this will be `smtp.mac.com`.

Enter the setup screen by pressing S at Pine's main menu. Then press C to enter the Config screen. To configure your email account, do the following:

1. Look at your email address. Set Pine's *user-domain* to everything after the @ symbol (for example, `mac.com`).

2. Set the *smtp-server* to your outgoing mail server (for example, `smtp.mac.com`).

3. Set your *inbox-path*:

    a. If you are using IMAP, set the inbox-path to {*incoming mail server/user=username*}inbox, as in {`mail.mac.com/user=dtaylor`}inbox.

    b. If you are using POP, set the inbox-path to {*incoming mail server/pop3/user=username*}*inbox*, as in {`pop3.nowhere.oreilly.com/pop3/user=dtaylor`}inbox.

The exact settings may vary. If you need more help, visit the Usenet newsgroup *comp.mail.pine* and look for the latest posting of the FAQ.

After you've made these changes, press E to exit Setup, press Y to commit changes, and then quit and restart Pine.

Reading email with Pine

When you first start Pine, the main menu appears, as shown earlier in Figure 9-12. You may also be prompted for your password, since Pine needs this to connect to your POP or IMAP server.

The highlighted line, which is the default command, gives a list of your email folders.* You can choose the highlighted command by pressing Return, pressing the greater-than sign (>), or typing the letter next to the command. (Here, this is l—a lowercase L. You don't need to type the commands in uppercase.) But because you probably haven't used Pine before, the only interesting folder is the inbox, which is the folder where your new messages wait for you to read them.

The display in Figure 9-13 shows that there are two messages waiting. Let's go directly to the inbox by pressing I (or by highlighting that line in the menu and pressing Return) to read the new mail. Figure 9-13 has the *message index* for our inbox.

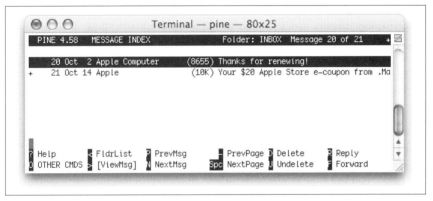

Figure 9-13. Pine message index

The main part of the window is a list of the messages in the folder, one message per line. If a line starts with N, it's a new message that hasn't been read. (The first message has been sitting in the inbox for some time now.) Next on each line is the *message number*; messages in a folder are numbered 1, 2, and so on. That's followed by the date the message was sent, who sent it, the number of characters in the message (size), and, finally, the message subject.

Let's skip the first message and read number 2. The down-arrow key or the N key moves the highlight bar over that message. As usual, you can get the default action—the one shown in brackets at the bottom of the display (here, [ViewMsg])—by pressing Return or >. The message from Apple will appear.

Just as > takes you forward in Pine, the < key generally takes you back to where you came from—in this case, the message index. You can type R to

---

* Pine also lets you read Usenet newsgroups. The L command takes you to another display where you choose the source of the folders, *then* you see the list of folders from that source.

reply to this message, F to forward it (send it on to someone else), D to mark it for deletion, and the Tab key to go to the next message without deleting this one.

When you mark a message for deletion, it stays in the folder message index, marked with a D at the left side of its line, until you quit Pine. Type Q to quit. Pine asks if you really want to quit. If you've marked messages for deletion, Pine asks if you want to *expunge* ("really delete") them. Answering Y here deletes the message.

Sending email with Pine

If you've already started Pine, you can compose a message from many of its displays by typing C. (Though, as always, not every Pine command is available at every display.) You can also start from the main menu. Or, at a shell prompt, you can go straight into message composition by typing pine *addr1 addr2*, where each *addr* is an email address such as *bjepson@oreilly.com*. In that case, after you've sent the mail message, Pine quits and leaves you at another shell prompt.

When you compose a message, Pine puts you in a window called the *composer*. (You'll also go into the composer if you use the Reply or Forward commands while you're reading another mail message.) The composer is a lot like another Unix text editor (Pico), but the first few lines are special because they're the message *header*—the "To:," "Cc:" (carbon copy), "Attchmnt:" (attached file), and "Subject:" lines. Figure 9-14 shows an example, already filled in.

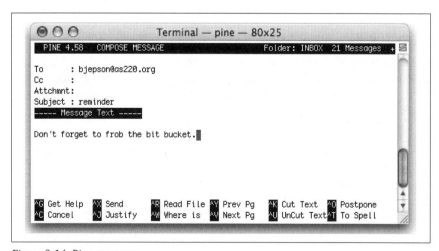

Figure 9-14. Pine composer

As you fill in the header, the composer works differently than when you're in the message text (body of the message). The list of commands at the bottom of the window is a bit different in those cases, too. For instance, while you edit the header, you can attach a file to the end of the message with the "Attach" command, which is Control-J. (Pine uses the ^ symbol to indicate a control character.) However, when you edit the body, you can read a file into the place you're currently editing (as opposed to attaching it) with the Control-R "Read File" command. But the main difference between editing the body and the header is the way you enter addresses.

If you have more than one address on the same line, separate them with commas (,). Pine will rearrange the addresses so there's just one on each line.

Move up and down between the header lines with Control-N and Control-P, or with the up-arrow and down-arrow keys. When you move into the message body (under the "Message Text" line), type any text you want. Paragraphs are usually separated with single blank lines.

 If you put a file in your home directory named *.signature* (the name starts with a dot (.), the composer automatically adds its contents to the end of every message you compose. (Some other Unix email programs work the same way.) It's good Internet etiquette to keep this file short—no more than four or five lines, if possible.

You can use editing commands such as Control-J to justify a paragraph and Control-T to check your spelling. When you're done, Control-X (exit) leaves the composer, asking first if you want to send the message you just wrote. Control-C cancels the message, though you'll be asked if you're sure. If you need to quit but don't want to send or cancel, the Control-O command postpones your message; then, the next time you try to start the composer, Pine asks whether you want to continue the postponed composition.

Editing Graphics with GIMP

GIMP (the GNU Image Manipulation Program) is a powerful free graphics manipulation program. You can get it at *http://www.gimp.org/*, and can use it to manipulate photos and other bitmap images in ways previously possible only with expensive graphics software.

To install GIMP, use the command `sudo apt-get install gimp` (see "Installing Packages," earlier in this chapter).

To run GIMP, you'll need to launch X11 and run the command `gimp &` at an xterm window. You can also add GIMP to the X11 Applications menu (see "Customizing the Applications Menu," earlier in this chapter). The first time you run GIMP, it will walk you through its user installation process (see Figure 9-15).

Figure 9-15. Installing GIMP for the first time

After you've finished setting GIMP up, several windows will appear, as shown in Figure 9-16. Clockwise from the top, they are:

Main Window and Toolbar

Use the menus in this window to open a file (File → Open), create a new file (File → New), or quit the GIMP (File → Quit). You can also select the active tool. Click this window to bring it to the front, and hover the mouse over the toolbar to see its name. Click a tool to select it.

Tool Options

Use this window to set configurable options for the current tool.

Brush Selection

Many tools, such as the paintbrush and eraser, use a certain brush shape. Use this window to select the brush properties.

Layers, Channels, and Paths

This Window lets you work with multilayered documents.

GIMP Tip of the Day

This window displays some helpful tips to help you use the GIMP.

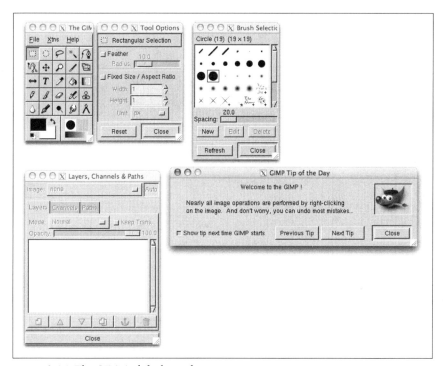

Figure 9-16. The GIMP's default windows

To open an existing file, select File → Open, and choose a file. Figure 9-17 shows a JPG picture open in the GIMP.

Figure 9-17. Editing a photograph in the GIMP

Command-Click or click the wedge in the upper-lefthand corner of the window to bring up a menu. The options are too numerous to describe completely, but the following list describes some you may find useful.

File → Save
    Save the file.

File → Revert
    Abandon all your changes and revert to the saved version.

Edit
    Contains the usual suspects: Undo, Redo, Cut, Copy, and Paste. It also includes Paste as New, which creates a new image out of whatever's in GIMP's clipboard.

Image → Scale Image
    Change the size of the image.

Image → Filters

Runs a filter over the image; you'll find filters that sharpen, despeckle, blur, and many more.

Script-Fu

Performs more complicated transformations to the image. You'll want to play around here, but be sure you are working on a backup copy. Figure 9-18 shows the result of the Alchemy → Predator transformation.

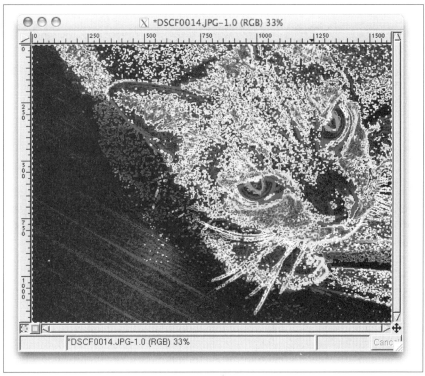

Figure 9-18. Transforming a predator with the Alchemy → Predator transformation

GIMP includes a set of extensions for generating various types of graphics, including buttons and logos. Switch to the GIMP main window and select Script-Fu from the Xtns menu (see Figure 9-19).

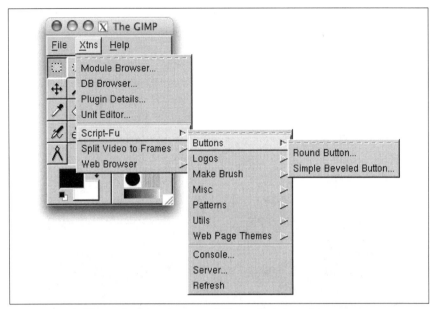

Figure 9-19. Exploring the Script-Fu options for generating graphics

The GIMP is a deep and broad application, and this section of the chapter has barely scratched the surface. You can use the GIMP to resize images, clear up red-eye (in your photos, that is; you're on your own for your own eyes), and perform sophisticated image enhancements. For more information on the GIMP, see the *GIMP Pocket Reference*, by Sven Neumann (O'Reilly).

## CHAPTER 10

Where to Go from Here

Now that you're almost to the end of this guide, let's look at some ways to continue learning about the Unix side of Mac OS X. Documentation is an obvious choice, but it isn't always in obvious places. You can also learn how to save time by taking advantage of other shell features—aliases, functions, and scripts—that let you shorten a repetitive job and "let the computer do the dirty work."

We'll close by seeing how you can use Unix commands on non-Unix systems.

Documentation

You might want to know the options to the programs we've introduced and get more information about them and the many other Unix programs. You're now ready to consult your system's documentation and other resources.

The man Command

Different versions of Unix have adapted Unix documentation in different ways. Almost all Unix systems have documentation derived from a manual originally called the *Unix Programmer's Manual*. The manual has numbered sections; each section is a collection of manual pages, often called manpages; each program has its own manpage. Section 1 has manpages for general Unix programs such as who and ls.

Mac OS X has individual manpages stored on the computer; users can read them online. If you want to know the correct syntax for entering a command or the particular features of a program, enter the command man and the name of the command. The syntax is:

```
man command
```

For example, if you want to find information about the program vi, which allows you to edit files, enter:

```
$ man vi
.
.
.
$
```

The output of man is filtered through the less pager in Mac OS X by default.

 Manpages are displayed using a program that doesn't write the displayed text to Terminal's scroll buffer. This can be quite annoying. Fortunately it's an easy fix: just specify PAGER="more" on the command line, or add the line export PAGER="more" to your ~/.bashrc, and the manpages will be left in the Terminal scroll buffer for later reference.

After you enter the command, the screen fills with text. Press the spacebar or Return to read more, and press q to quit.

Mac OS X also includes a command called apropos, or man -k, to help you locate a command if you have an idea of what it does but are not sure of its correct name. Enter apropos followed by a descriptive word; you'll get a list of commands that might help. To get this working, however, you need to first build the apropos database. This is done when Mac OS X runs its weekly maintenance job, which can be run manually with the following command:

```
$ sudo periodic weekly
Password:
$
```

Don't be surprised if it takes ten minutes or longer for the periodic command to complete; it's doing quite a lot of work in the background. Once complete, you can use apropos to find all commands related to PostScript, for example, with:

```
$ man -k postscript
enscript(1)          - convert text files to PostScript
grops(1)             - PostScript driver for groff
pfbtops(1)           - translate a PostScript font in .pfb format to ASCII
pstopdf(1)           - convert PostScript input into a PDF document
```

Problem checklist

man says there is no manual entry for the command.

Some commands—cd and jobs, for example—aren't separate Unix programs; they're part of the shell. On Mac OS X, you'll find the documentation for those commands in the manual page for bash.

If the program isn't a standard part of your Unix system—that is, you or your system staff added the program to your system—there may not be a manual page, or you may have to configure the man program to find the local manpage files.

The third possibility is that you don't have all the manpage directories in your MANPATH variable. If so, add the following to your *.bashrc* (see "Creating and Editing Files" in Chapter 4), then open a new Terminal window for the settings to take effect:

```
export MANPATH=/sw/share/man:/sw/man:${MANPATH}:/usr/X11R6/man
```

Documentation Via the Internet

The Internet changes so quickly that any list of online Unix documentation we'd give you would soon be out of date. Still, the Internet is a great place to find out about Unix systems. Remember that there are many different versions of Unix, so some documentation you find may not be completely right for you. Also, some information you'll find may be far too technical for your needs (many computer professionals use and discuss Unix). But don't be discouraged! Once you've found a site with the general kind of information you want, you can probably come back later for more.

The premier place to start your exploration of online documentation for Mac OS X Unix is the Apple web site. But don't start on their home page. Start either on their Mac OS X page (*http://www.apple.com/macosx/*) or their Darwin project home page (*http://developer.apple.com/darwin/*). Another excellent place to get information about software downloads and add-ons to your Unix world is the Fink project (see "Fink" in Chapter 9).

Many Unix command names are plain English words, which can make searching hard. If you're looking for collections of Unix information, try searching for the Unix program named grep. One especially Unix-friendly search engine is Google, at *http://www.google.com*. Google offers a specialized Macintosh search engine at *http://www.google.com/mac* and a BSD search engine at *http://www.google.com/bsd* (which is useful because Mac OS X's Unix personality derives from its BSD heritage).

Here are some other places to try:

Magazines
> Some print and online magazines have Unix tutorials and links to more information. Macintosh magazines include MacTech (*http://www.mactech.com*), MacWorld (*http://www.macworld.com*), and Mac-Addict (*http://www.macaddict.com*).

Publishers

Publishers such as O'Reilly & Associates, Inc. (*http://www.oreilly.com*) have areas of their web sites that feature Unix and have articles written by their books' authors. They may also have books online (such as the O'Reilly Safari service) available for a small monthly fee—which is a good way to learn a lot quickly without needing to buy a paper copy of a huge book, most of which you might not need.

Universities

Many schools use Unix-like systems and will have online documentation. You'll probably have better luck at the Computer Services division (which services the whole campus) than at the Computer Science department (which may be more technical).

Mac OS X–related web sites

Many Mac OS X web sites are worthy of note, though they're run by third parties and may change by the time you read this. Mac OS X Apps (*http://www.macosxapps.com*) offers a wide variety of Aqua applications. Information on Darwin can be found at Open Darwin (*http://www.opendarwin.org*), and Mac OS X Hints (*http://www.macosxhints.com*) offers valuable information and hints. One more site well worth a bookmark is O'Reilly's MacDevCenter (*http://www.macdevcenter.com/*).

User Groups

Apple User Groups are an excellent source of information, inspiration, and camaraderie. To find an Apple User Group near you, see *http://www.apple. com/usergroups/*.

Books

Bookstores, both traditional and online, are full of computer books. The books are written for a wide variety of needs and backgrounds. Unfortunately, many books are rushed to press, written by authors with minimal Unix experience, and full of errors. Before you buy a book, read through parts of it. Does the style (brief or lots of detail, chatty and friendly or organized as a reference) fit your needs? Search the Internet for reviews; online bookstores may have readers' comments on file.

Shell Aliases and Functions

If you type command names that are hard for you to remember, or command lines that seem too long, you'll want to learn about *shell aliases* and *shell functions*. These shell features let you abbreviate commands, command lines, and long series of commands. In most cases, you can replace them with a single word or a word and a few arguments. For example, one of the long pipelines (see the section "Pipes and Filters" in Chapter 6) could be replaced by an alias or function (for instance, aug). When you type aug at a shell prompt, the shell would list files modified in August, sorted by size.

Making an alias or function is almost as simple as typing in the command line or lines that you want to run. References in the section "Documentation" earlier in this chapter, have more information. Shell aliases and functions are actually a simple case of shell programming. For more information on aliases, see "Creating Aliases" in Chapter 1.

Programming

We mention earlier that the shell is the system's command interpreter. It reads each command line you enter at your terminal and performs the operation that you call for. Your shell is chosen when your account is set up.

The shell is just an ordinary program that can be called by a Unix command. However, it contains some features (such as variables, control structures, and so on) that make it similar to a programming language. You can save a series of shell commands in a file, called a *shell script*, to accomplish specialized functions.

Programming the shell should be attempted only when you are reasonably confident in your ability to use Unix commands. Unix is quite a powerful tool, and its capabilities become more apparent when you try your hand at shell programming.

Take time to learn the basics. Then, when you're faced with a new task, take time to browse through references to find programs or options that will help you get the job done more easily. Once you've done that, learn how to build shell scripts so that you never have to type a complicated command sequence more than once.

Let's have a closer look at a shell script to give you some flavor of what can be done. First, to list all known user accounts on the system, you need to extract the information from the NetInfo database, which can be done by using nireport.

 You can try this script, listusers, by entering the following few lines into vi, pico, or another editor of your choice. See Chapter 4 for additional information on editing files.

```
#!/bin/sh

echo "UID       NAME    FULLNAME       HOME           SHELL"

nireport . /users uid name realname home shell | \
    awk '$1 > 99 { print $0 }'
```

The first line indicates what program should run the script, and, like most scripts, this is written for the Bourne Shell, /bin/sh. By using the awk utility to test for user IDs greater than 99, this script further screens out any account information for system accounts (which, by convention, have an ID value of less than 100).

To make a shell script act as if it's a new program rather than just a text file, you use chmod +x to make it executable, then you can run it by typing in its name if it's in your current PATH (see Chapter 1 for more information on setting and customizing your PATH), or with the ./ prefix to indicate that it's in the current directory, as shown here:

```
$ chmod +x listusers
$ ./listusers
UID    NAME    FULLNAME     HOME           SHELL
501    taylor  Dave Taylor  /Users/taylor  /bin/bash
502    tintin  Mr. Tintin   /Users/tintin  /bin/bash
```

This is really the tip of the iceberg with shell scripts. For more information, look at *Unix in a Nutshell*, by Arnold Robbins, and *Unix Power Tools*, by Shelley Powers, Jerry Peek, Tim O'Reilly, and Mike Loukides (both published by O'Reilly), or *Wicked Cool Shell Scripts*, by Dave Taylor (NoStarch Press).

Shell Scripts into Droplets

Another very cool trick with Mac OS X is to turn a shell script into a droplet, an application that can be have files dropped onto it from the Finder. To do this, you'll need to have a script to download and launch a copy of Fred Sanchez' DropScript utility.

Get DropScript by going to *http://www.versiontracker.com/* and searching for "dropscript." VersionTracker is well worth exploring too, helping you keep up-to-date on system and application updates.

At its simplest, a droplet script accepts one or more files, which are given as command-line arguments, which are then processed in some manner. As a simple example, here's a droplet script that prints whatever files you give it:

```
#!/bin/sh
pr "$*" | lpr
```

This can be turned into a droplet by dragging the shell script icon over the DropScript application in the Finder. It creates a new version called drop*filename* that's fully drag-and-drop–enabled. For example, if this script were called print-text, the droplet would be called dropprint-text.

More Possibilities: Perl and Python

If shell script programming seems too limiting, you might want to learn Perl or Python. Like the shell, Perl and Python interpret script files full of commands. But these two programming languages have a steeper learning curve than the shell. Also, because you've already learned a fair amount about the shell and Unix commands by reading this book, you're almost ready to start writing shell scripts now; on the other hand, a programming language will take longer to learn. But if you have sophisticated needs, learning one of these languages is another way to use even more of the power of your Mac OS X system.

Index

Symbols

& (ampersand), specifying background
    process, 98
* (asterisk)
    in regular expressions, 94
    indicating executable file, 43
    wildcard, 59
\ (backslash)
    before spaces in pathname, 35
    prefacing spaces and special
        characters, 58
: (colon)
    in filenames or directory names, 57
    prompt for less command, 95
- (dash)
    in command line, 27
    indicating plain file in listing, 41
-- (dash, double) in command line, 27
$ (dollar sign)
    at end of prompt, 15, 22
    command, vi, 64
$$ (dollar sign, double), PID of current
    shell, 102
.. (dot dot), indicating parent
    directory, 36
. (dot), indicating working directory, 40
! escape sequence, 15
\$ escape sequence, 16
\@ escape sequence, 15
^[escape sequence, 17

>> (greater-than symbol, double), as
    append redirection
    operator, 91
> (greater-than symbol), sending output
    to file, 87, 88–91
(hash mark), at end of prompt, 22
? (help) command, Pine, 138
< (less-than symbol), getting input from
    a file, 87
% (percent sign) prompt, 15
| (pipe operator), 87, 92
? (question mark) wildcard, 59
"" (quotes)
    around filenames with spaces, 27
    around pathnames with spaces, 35
; (semicolon), on command line, 28
/ (slash)
    in pathname, 35
    indicating directory in listing, 43
    indicating root directory, 33, 36
    starting pattern in vi, 64, 66
[] (square brackets) wildcards, 59
~ (tilde), indicating home directory, 69

Numbers

0 command, vi, 64
1 command, vi, 66

We'd like to hear your suggestions for improving our indexes. Send email to *index@oreilly.com*.

H

H command, vi, 64
h command, vi, 64, 66
\H escape sequence, 15
\h escape sequence, 15
hackers, 110
hard links, 76
hash command, ftp, 113
hash mark (#), at end of prompt, 22
help (?) command, Pine, 138
help command, ftp, 114
HFS metadata, 71
hidden files, 40
history of commands, 15, 16
  (see also scroll buffer)
home directory, 33, 69
hostname, displaying in prompt, 15
hung session, 30
hyphen (-)
  in command line, 27
  indicating plain file in listing, 41

I

i command, vi, 63, 66
I (inbox) command, Pine, 141
icewm window manager, 120
iDisk, mounting, 34
input/output redirection (see I/O
    redirection)
Insert mode, vi, 62
interactive Unix programs, 29
Internet (see network access; web sites)
interpreted programs, 102
I/O redirection, 87
IP address, for remote access, 107

J

j command, vi, 64, 66
Jepson, Brian (Mac OS X Panther for
    Unix Geeks), 3
job control, 97, 98, 103
jobs
  errors regarding, 26
  running in background (see
      background process)
  suspending, 30
jobs command, 30, 103

K

k command, vi, 64, 66
keyboard, as standard input, 87
Keyboard settings in Terminal
    Inspector, 11
keys, changing function of, 11
kill command, 30, 98, 103
ksh (Korn shell), 22

L

l command, vi, 64
"l", indicating link in listing, 55
Lamb, Linda (Learning the vi
    Editor), 65
lcd command, ftp, 114
Learning the bash Shell (Newham;
    Rosenblatt), 12, 19
Learning the Unix Operating System
    (Peek; Todina; Strang), xiii
Learning the vi Editor (Lamb;
    Robbins), 65
Left Arrow key, 25
less command, 13, 14, 46, 95
LESS environment variable, 13, 14, 47
less-than symbol (<), getting input from
    a file, 87
links, 76
  creating, 75
  indicated in listing, 55
  number of, 41
  (see also aliases)
Linux, ix
Linux Printing archive, 79
ln command, 75
locate command, 73
logging out of session, 25
logins, remote, 105–108
Loukides, Mike (Unix Power Tools), 19,
    154
lpq command, 83
lpr command, 82, 85
lprm command, 84
ls command, 28, 40–43
Lynx web browser, 135–137

M

m2u command, 61
Mac OS X, vii
  book about, xi
  editors included with, 60

superuser, 22, 54
(see also accounts; permissions)
/Users/Shared directory, 48
UTF-8 encoding, 8

V

VersionTracker software, 119
vertical bar (|), as pipe operator, 87, 92
vi Editor Pocket Reference
    (Robbins), 65
vi text editor, 62–66
vim text editor, 62
Virtual Network Computer (VNC), 127
VNC (Virtual Network Computer), 127
/Volumes directory, 35, 55, 78
VT-100 emulation, 6

W

:w command, vi, 65, 66
w command, vi, 66
\W escape sequence, 15
\w escape sequence, 15
W (Whereis) command, Pine, 138
w (write permission), 42
web browser
    FTP used with, 115
    Lynx, 135–137
web server, accessing, 107
web sites
    Apple Developer Connection
        (ADC), 70
    Apple User Groups, 152
    Darwin project, ix, 151
    DarwinPorts project, ix
    DropScript utility, 154
    Fink installer, 131
    FinkCommander application, 133
    for this book, xii
    FTP programs, 116
    GIMP application, 143
    Google search engine, 151
    Mac OS X, 151, 152
    Mac OS X Apps, 152
    Mac OS X Hints, 152
    MacDevCenter, 152
    Macintosh magazines, 151
    online documentation, 151
    Open Darwin, 152
    OpenSSH, 105

O'Reilly & Associates, Inc., xiii
printer drivers, 79
PuTTY, 105
remote login programs, 105
Share My Desktop application, 127
SourceForge, ix
SSH, 105
StarOffice application, 125
VersionTracker software, 119
VNC (Virtual Network
    Computer), 127
X11 FAQ, 124
XFree86, 120
who command, 23, 28
Wicked Cool Shell Scripts (Taylor), 12
wildcards in filenames or directory
    names, 59
window managers for X11, 120
Window settings for Terminal
    Inspector, 9
windows
    as standard output, 87
    clearing or redrawing, 30
    closing, 31
    closing preferences for, 4, 5
    Command Key option for, 10
    cycling between open windows, 21
    opening as .term files, 18
    opening multiple windows, 21
    prompting before closing, 5
    saving configuration of as .term
        file, 18
    scroll buffer for (see scroll buffer)
    size of, 9
    title of, 10, 17
    transparency of, 8
Windows operating system, accessing
    files on, 78
word processors, 62
    (see also OpenOffice.org application)
working directory, 33
    changing, 38
    displaying, 37
    displaying in prompt, 15
    in file listing, 40
:wq command, vi, 66
write permission, 42
    for directory, 48
    for files, 48

X

X clients, 119
X command, vi, 66
x command, vi, 65, 66
x (execute permission), 42
X servers, 119
X (Set/Unset) command, Pine, 139
X Window System (see X11 application)
X11 application, 119–121
    application menus in, 123
    applications in, 121–123, 124
    Applications menu in, 125
    .bashrc file and, 124
    c-Q command in, 123
    cutting and pasting with, 123
    FAQ for, 124
    installing, 121
    OpenOffice.org application and, 125
    private network remote access
        and, 129
    .profile file ignored in, 124
    remote access from, 126–130
    running on other computers, 130
    scrolling xterm with, 123
    starting, 121
xcalc application, X11, 122
xclock application, X11, 121
XCode, 70
xeyes application, X11, 122
XFree86, 120
xhost application, X11, 122
xkill application, X11, 122
xload application, X11, 123
xman application, X11, 121

Y

y1 command, vi, 65
ynw command, vi, 65
yw command, vi, 65, 66
yy command, vi, 65, 66

Z

zsh (Z shell), 22
ZZ command, vi, 66

About the Author

Dave Taylor is a popular writer, teacher, and speaker focused on business and technology issues. He is the founder of The Internet Mall and *iTrack.com* and has been involved with Unix and the Internet since 1980, having created the popular Elm mail system. He's also been a Mac fan since its original release, when he started out with a dirty beige Mac Plus. Previous positions include being a research scientist at HP Laboratories and senior reviews editor of *SunWorld* magazine. He has contributed software to the official 4.4 release of Berkeley Unix (BSD), and his programs are found in all versions of Linux and other popular Unix variants.

Brian Jepson is an O'Reilly editor, programmer, and coauthor of *Mac OS X for Unix Geeks* and *Learning Unix for Mac OS X*. He's also a volunteer system administrator and all-around geek for AS220 (*http://www.as220.org*), a nonprofit arts center in Providence, RI. AS220 gives Rhode Island artists uncensored and unjuried forums for their work. These forums include galleries, performance space, and publications. Brian sees to it that technology, especially free software, supports that mission.

Colophon

Our look is the result of reader comments, our own experimentation, and feedback from distribution channels. Distinctive covers complement our distinctive approach to technical topics, breathing personality and life into potentially dry subjects.

The animal on the cover of *Learning Unix for Mac OS X Panther* is an Alaskan malamute. The Alaskan malamute is one of the oldest Arctic sled dogs. These powerful dogs have muscular bodies, structured for strength and endurance. They have broad heads with bulky muzzles and triangular ears, which stand erect to signify alertness. Their thick coats are coarse and dark on the outside, with soft, woolly undercoats.

Alaskan malamutes make excellent companions, as they are affectionate, friendly, and loyal. They can be playful, but tend to become more reserved as they mature. They are very intelligent, with eyes that reveal their curiosity and interest.

Mary Brady was the production editor and copyeditor for *Learning Unix for Mac OS X Panther*. Leanne Soylemez was the proofreader. Sarah Sherman and Claire Cloutier provided quality control. Angela Howard wrote the index.

Emma Colby designed the cover of this book, based on a series design by Edie Freedman. The cover image is an illustration from the *Illustrated Natural History: Mammalia*. Emma Colby produced the cover layout and the quick reference card with QuarkXPress 4.1 using Adobe's ITC Garamond, Myriad Condensed, and Linotype Birka fonts.

David Futato designed the interior layout. This book was converted by Julie Hawks to FrameMaker 5.5.6 with a format conversion tool created by Erik Ray, Jason McIntosh, Neil Walls, and Mike Sierra that uses Perl and XML technologies. The text font is Linotype Birka; the heading font is Adobe Myriad Condensed; and the code font is LucasFont's TheSans Mono Condensed. The illustrations that appear in the book were produced by Robert Romano and Jessamyn Read using Macromedia FreeHand 9 and Adobe Photoshop 6. The tip and warning icons were drawn by Christopher Bing. This colophon was written by Linley Dolby.

Related Titles Available from O'Reilly

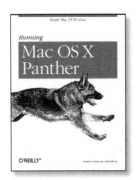

Macintosh

AppleScript: The Definitive Guide

Appleworks 6: The Missing Manual

The Best of the Joy of Tech

iMovie 3 and iDVD: The Missing Manual

iPhoto2: The Missing Manual

iPod & iTunes: The Missing Manual, *2nd Edition*

Mac OS X Panther in a Nutshell

Mac OS X Panther Pocket Guide

Mac OS X: The Missing Manual, *Panther Edition*

Mac OS X Unwired

Macintosh Troubleshooting Pocket Guide

Office X for the Macintosh: The Missing Manual

Running Mac OS X Panther

Mac Developers

Building Cocoa Applications: A Step-By-Step Guide

Cocoa in a Nutshell

Learning Carbon

Learning Cocoa with Objective-C, *2nd Edition*

Mac OS X for Java Geeks

Mac OS X Hacks

Mac OS X Panther Hacks

Mac OS X Panther for Unix Geeks

Objective-C Pocket Reference

RealBasic: The Definitive Guide, *2nd Edition*

Keep in touch with O'Reilly

1. Download examples from our books

To find example files for a book, go to:
www.oreilly.com/catalog
select the book, and follow the "Examples" link.

2. Register your O'Reilly books

Register your book at *register.oreilly.com*

Why register your books? Once you've registered your O'Reilly books you can:

- Win O'Reilly books, T-shirts or discount coupons in our monthly drawing.
- Get special offers available only to registered O'Reilly customers.
- Get catalogs announcing new books (US and UK only).
- Get email notification of new editions of the O'Reilly books you own.

3. Join our email lists

Sign up to get topic-specific email announcements of new books and conferences, special offers, and O'Reilly Network technology newsletters at:

elists.oreilly.com

It's easy to customize your free elists subscription so you'll get exactly the O'Reilly news you want.

4. Get the latest news, tips, and tools

http://www.oreilly.com

- "Top 100 Sites on the Web"—PC Magazine
- CIO Magazine's Web Business 50 Awards

Our web site contains a library of comprehensive product information (including book excerpts and tables of contents), downloadable software, background articles, interviews with technology leaders, links to relevant sites, book cover art, and more.

5. Work for O'Reilly

Check out our web site for current employment opportunities:

jobs.oreilly.com

6. Contact us

O'Reilly & Associates
1005 Gravenstein Hwy North
Sebastopol, CA 95472 USA

TEL: 707-827-7000 or 800-998-9938
(6am to 5pm PST)

FAX: 707-829-0104

order@oreilly.com
For answers to problems regarding your order or our products.
To place a book order online, visit:

www.oreilly.com/order_new

catalog@oreilly.com
To request a copy of our latest catalog.

booktech@oreilly.com
For book content technical questions or corrections.

corporate@oreilly.com
For educational, library, government, and corporate sales.

proposals@oreilly.com
To submit new book proposals to our editors and product managers.

international@oreilly.com
For information about our international distributors or translation queries. For a list of our distributors outside of North America check out:

international.oreilly.com/distributors.html

adoption@oreilly.com
For information about academic use of O'Reilly books, visit:

academic.oreilly.com

O'REILLY®

Our books are available at most retail and online bookstores.
To order direct: 1-800-998-9938 • *order@oreilly.com* • *www.oreilly.com*
Online editions of most O'Reilly titles are available by subscription at *safari.oreilly.com*